HOW TO GET SUPER RICH IN THE OPPORTUNITY MARKET!

BY T.J. ROHLEDER

Also by T.J. Rohleder:

The Black Book of Marketing Secrets (Series)
The Ultimate Wealth-Maker
Four Magical Secrets to Building a Fabulous Fortune
The Ruthless Marketing Attack
$60,000.00 in 90 Days
How to Start Your Own Million Dollar Business
Fast Track to Riches
Five Secrets That Will Triple Your Profits
25 Direct Mail Success Secrets That Can Make You Rich
24 Simple and Easy Ways to Get Rich Quick
How to Create a Hot Selling Internet Product in One Day
Secrets of the Blue Jeans Millionaire
Shortcut Secrets to Creating High-Profit Products

FIRST EDITION

ISBN 1-933356-05-7

Table of Contents

Introduction

Would you like to become a successful entrepreneur? Would you like to create products and relationships that can earn you millions of dollars? Would you like to set up a legion of business and joint venture partners to rapidly grow your business? **Then hold on, because you're about to go on a wild ride through a truly remarkable American success story -- if I do say so myself!** Welcome to How to Get Super Rich in the Opportunity Market!

My name is T.J. Rohleder, and I'm the co-founder of a business called M.O.R.E., Inc., located in the little town of Goessel, Kansas. In my 20 years in the business, I've marketed hundreds of informational products that I've either created on my own or created jointly with other entrepreneurs. Recently, I had the privilege and the pleasure to sit down and speak with Mike Lamb, the host of a top-notch radio program called Money Room. **He's interviewed hundreds of entrepreneurs, Internet marketers, authors, and business professionals and our own conversation lasted for hours.** *This book is adapted from an audio presentation based on that interview.*

I believe that this is an exciting book because it chronicles the details of our success at M.O.R.E., Inc., revealing a lot of our business secrets along the way. **As Mike put it (and I blush to repeat), for the last two decades, my wife Eileen and I, along with our mentors and our staff and a host of joint venture partners, have written an unbelievable success story.** Mike was interested in learning how we did it so he encouraged me to take a break from my schedule, to sit down, and do a 10-hour interview series. That's the genesis of this book. In these pages, you'll learn how Eileen and I got started, how we grew our empire, how we developed these opportunities, why our customers love us so much, and how we've been able to produce such an amazing array of products.

You're about to get a firsthand account of how my mind works. I'll show you how you can use my knowledge, my insight, my experience, my failures, and my enormous successes to create your own fortune in the opportunity market. All you have to do is read on, absorb these concepts, and apply them to your business.

So jump right in -- because there's plenty of room here at the top.

Chapter One

Getting Started

Mike Lamb likes to tell the story about the day, back when he was first starting out, that he bought an audio program called The $2,500 Weekend at a garage sale for a couple of dollars. This is a tape series that my wife Eileen, our mentor Russ von Hoelscher, and I put together years and years ago. It wasn't our first product, but it was one of the first few. Mike's copy was missing Tape No. 4 and it was about 15 years before I replaced it for him.

Sixteen years after creating that product, we're still duplicating thousands of sets every year, in both audiocassette and CD formats. I find it amazing that this sort of information is so evergreen in nature that it continues to be valuable as time goes by, but that's one of the great things about this business. **You do something once -- in that case, over the course of a weekend -- and it just keeps selling at an amazing rate**. We did over $1.5 million in sales on that single product. And now we use it as a bonus gift for many of our newer products. We use it both as a way of helping to educate some of our new customers and as a calling card. It helps them get to know us a little bit. They can hear for themselves who we are and where we're from.

Not much has changed in this business over the past few decades. The trends are pretty much the same; it's ebb and flow. **People are always looking to find new ways to make more money.** Hence the idea behind this book and the radio program it's based on. The opportunity market is a marketplace that was there 100 years ago, it'll be there 100 years from now, and it'll be here

200 years from now. It'll probably be around for as long as human beings are. That's one of the exciting things that gets me out of bed every morning: I realize that no matter what the economy does, this is a marketplace that's going to continue to rock 'n roll. **This is a marketplace that's always going to be profitable**, simply because of the huge demand.

One of the things that makes it exciting is the Baby Boomers generation (of which I'm a part). We're starting to get old enough to retire -- and my fellow Boomers see that the window is closing for them to make enough money to retire on. They're running out of time, so they're going to be frantically searching for a way to make that money. I believe that the best years in the opportunity market are the next decade or two, as those Baby Boomers get up there and start searching for some way to make more money with less work.

I've been involved with a lot of people over the years. My wife Eileen and I started with $300 dollars back in 1988. We got that money from selling a beat-up old carpet-cleaning van that ran on only five of its six cylinders and was parked in our backyard, collecting dust. Our first ad was a hit right out of the gate -- and do you know why that is? **It's because, for years, we were our own best customers.** We were sending away for all kinds of programs in the opportunity market, so we had an excellent feel for the marketplace right from the start, without even realizing it. We bought one ad and it immediately made enough of a profit that we could buy two ads. We took the profits from those and then we bought four ads and eight ads and so on.

Eileen and I had a great partnership -- and we still do, even though she hasn't had much to do with the business now for about seven years. She had to step down for health reasons in 2001, but she ran the company for the first 13-14 years we were in business. If it weren't for her, nothing would have ever happened. I was too young, too immature to succeed on my own; I would have blown the whole thing up because I was too wild and crazy, but she has a lot of common sense. So Eileen deserves a lot of the credit for our success. So does Russ von Hoelscher. After pulling in about $16,000 a month during the first six months of our business, we had the good fortune to meet Russ, who is a marketing expert. Russ helped Eileen and I go from $16,000 a month to almost $100,000 a week in the first nine months he worked with us!

So, yeah, it was a wild roller coaster ride. Here we were, little "Forrest Gumps" from small-town America who had never made more than $28,000 a year -- and that's counting both of our incomes together. **Within six months of running our first ad, though, we were hitting five figures -- and again, a lot of that's because of Eileen**. Some of my initial ideas were kind of stupid, they never would have worked. She talked me out of them and we went **with the better ideas in the beginning. Then we met Russ and he helped us turn our $300 investment into over $10 million in our first four years.** I'm always going to be indebted to Russ. He's a great guy, super smart. Then, in 1993, we met Dan Kennedy -- and between Russ von Hoelscher and Dan, we catapulted our business into the stratosphere.

Dan Kennedy is another mentor who's helped us a great deal, a person who's put millions and millions of dollars into our pockets. We were part of his Platinum Group for nearly six years and that was instrumental to our success.

We met Alan R. Bechtold in 1996 and Alan helped us get involved with the Internet. We've made millions of dollars with the Internet since. Then, over a period of time, we've developed a group called the $100,000,000 Roundtable, which consists of a number of sharp marketers whose ambitions lie in the same directions ours do. There have been anywhere from 10 to 15 different members in that group over the last decade.

Mike Lamb's a member, so is my son-in-law Chris Lakey, who's been in and around the business for over half of his life. Then there are people like Don Bice, Jeff Gardner, Eric R. Bechtold, Ken Pederson, Bill Glazer, Randy Charach, Chris Hollinger, Ted Ciuba, Gary Halbert, and Jay Abraham who have also been members, not to mention legendary marketers Dan Kennedy and Jeff Paul.

I wanted to get these acknowledgements out of the way, first, because there are two things that I ask people to write down every time we give a seminar. **One is the fact that no one gets rich by accident, there's always a reason.** Even if people think they got lucky and stumbled onto their success, there's still a reason why they got rich. **Number Two: nobody gets rich by themselves.** It's the people you surround yourself with that make all the difference. My wife Eileen put together a great staff of people in our company. I took over seven years ago and haven't let them off yet.

Entrepreneurs like to pretend sometimes -- they want people to believe that they've done it all themselves, that they're super people who don't need any help from anyone. That's just not true. **It's always the people behind the scenes who make a difference.** I've had a lot of help from a lot of people and I want to point that out immediately -- because I know my readers have high ambitions. They want to get rich. After all, only a fool would invest in a book called How to Get Super Rich in the Opportunity Market if they didn't! **But I see far too many smart people who never make money.** They have all kinds of talents and abilities that I'll never have and they're a lot smarter than I'll ever be, but their I.Q. can be a curse when it comes to amassing riches. I've had the good fortune of meeting numerous people who have a net worth in the $50-100 million range. The more you get to know these people, the more you find out that they've had the same staff with them for 20 or 25 years. They've been doing business with the same people for decade after decade. **They've built relationships that have played a major role in their success.** This is a community. You invite people into your community and, if things work out, you not only make money together, you essentially have a symphony of information on your hands.

Everybody does their part and, yes, not everybody is as smart as the next person. **There's a learning curve, obviously, and, as the poet John Donne famously put it, "No man is an island."** I've never understood why some business people believe they can do it all themselves. I've found that there's no way I, personally, can do it all. I don't want to do it all. When you get right down to it, I'm a lazy guy. I'd rather sit back and create something, or have something created for me, and then go out and use my skills and my talent toward making that product a success.

The best partnerships are those in which people bring complimentary skills and abilities into the mix. So, you have to know where your strengths and weaknesses are and then you have to find as many other people as you can to slot in there to fill the gaps. Plus, there's all kinds of new knowledge that you can acquire from people who have gone before you and that's why being involved with things like Dan Kennedy's Platinum Group and my $100,000,000 Roundtable is important. Being part of a group of people who are smart and experienced, who have the knowledge and are kicking ideas around constantly, and being exposed to different opinions from people who have gone where you want to go and who have done what you're trying to do -- that can be crucial to turning small sums of money into a fortune.

Years ago, I was told that you become one with the people you associate with -- so if you really want to be successful, hang out with successful people and learn all that you can. And another point that I want to make here is that there are many, many things that we have to do in marketing and business that aren't fun. **So**

---

why would you want to do something that you don't like to do? **Find somebody who enjoys that element, who has that skill set, and let them do it.** I like what Dan Kennedy says. He says that when he goes to the bank to make his daily deposit, they don't ask him, "Now, Dan, did you have to work your ass off to get this money?" There's such a thing as working smart. You find out what you're best at, you put your focus there, and try to find other people who are good at the things you're not good at -- and that does create a synergistic effort if you work it right.

Getting Started

Depending on your experience level, this book may be the beginning of a very large, lengthy educational process. But just take all these pieces of information as they come and put them away until you need them. **You don't have to try to apply everything at once; in fact, you probably shouldn't.** You can very easily start doing things on a small scale, just like my wife and I did. Don't let the options -- and there are a lot of them! -- overwhelm you. **We started with something that you can still start with today and that's the concept of small ads.** Sure, it's not very romantic. It doesn't have all the bells and whistles that other marketing options do and it's not new and exciting. But when people ask me the best way to get started in this business, I tell them to run space advertising. It's often overlooked in favor of the new, modern high tech that we love so much. All that does offer hope and promise, but there's nothing like a little tiny space advertisement. It's the most risk-free way to make money.

The only negative aspects are twofold. Number One, you won't get rich running little ads -- unless of course you have thousands of them out there. I do know some people who are making millions of dollars running small space ads, but they're running in thousands and thousands of newspapers every week and

---

every available magazine that they can buy media space in. <u>So you're never really going to get rich unless you expand it in the largest way, but what you're going to do is limit all of your risks.</u> **Those tiny ads will almost always make a profit, so you don't have to worry about losing money.** And you can pyramid your advertising; as I said earlier, that's what we did. We took out a $300 ad, then we took the profits and put it into two more ads and then we took that profit and bought two more, until finally we had a nice little foundation to build on. Before we met Russ von Hoelscher, we were bringing in a tidy $16,000 dollars a month.

I think people are all in love with all of the whiz-bang options out there, whereas what they should do is focus on the tried-and-true methods in the beginning. Once they've got a foundation laid out, they can start experimenting with all the new stuff. **The tried-and-true may not be glamorous, but it offers profit with minimal risk. Not only that, but you also start building a list that you can continue to build on, <u>developing real relationships with real people</u>.** That's crucial in this marketplace. If I had to boil my success down to a single secret, it would have to be building relationships. It all starts with people who buy from you one time. You treat them right, make them happy, and starting building your relationship from there. Because this is a marketplace where people are very hungry, where they're obsessed with finding a good way to make money, they'll buy from you and again and again if you value them and treat them right.

Ironically, these same customers are also very skeptical -- going into it, you have to realize just how skeptical this marketplace is. But when they know they can trust you, when you sell them something and prove that it's something of value, they will gladly come back to you -- rather than having to do business with somebody new that they don't have a relationship with.

Now, let's get back to those display ads. They don't have

---

to be big; the size depends entirely on how much money you have. If you're really broke, there's nothing like the lowly little tiny classified advertisement. We started with one that was one-sixth the size of a standard display ad, and that's a nice size when you're new.

The magazine we started in no longer exists; it was a good one, but opportunity magazines come and go. You have to keep an eye on what's out there. The market is constantly changing; there are always new publications coming in and old ones going out. **The best way to learn to write your own ads for the opportunity market is to do what we did when we started out: become an opportunity junkie!** When we got started, we were already customers of a lot of the companies we were competing against -- so we already had real, intimate knowledge of the marketplace. <u>Because we were customers, we really had a feel for what was out there and, when it came time to developing our own offers, we knew what excited us the most</u>. That it made it easy to develop an offer that we knew was good. We'd actually tested out and failed at a bunch of different things by then. **What we did was take a couple of the best ideas that we had from other people and mixed them together to create our own book.**

So, get a feel for the marketplace. Send away for a hundred different things that are being sold in the opportunity market. Go to the back of the tabloids. Write to every one of the companies that has something that appeals to you. Go to USA Today; they've got a great ad section, especially in their weekend edition. Go to Popular Mechanics. Send away for the best opportunities you see. Watch your mailbox and, pretty soon, your name's going to end up on a bunch of mailing lists. **All you have to do is send for a hundred opportunities and for the rest of your life you're going to be getting opportunity mail from a wide variety of different sources**. Keep studying it, taking notes, internalizing it, and you'll get a feel for it.

You may be thinking, "But all that's junk mail!" Not to you, it isn't. You need to embrace it; this is a learning experience. **Here's an opportunity for you to get on all these mailing lists and have people send you their marketing material so you can see what they're doing and what the trends are.** It's a free way of learning the secrets of the opportunity marketing field. This is an easy way to get on the other side of the cash register.

You stop thinking like a consumer and you start realizing that all that mail that's coming through your mailbox is making a profit for the companies that have been in business for any length of time -- or they wouldn't keep sending it out, now would they?

Armed with that knowledge, knowing now that you want to be in that same market, start studying all these great ads. Look for certain themes. You'll see certain common denominators that I'm going to talk about in detail in this book. There's no better knowledge than that.

That first little ad that Eileen and I put together -- now, I told you that was a $300 advertisement. **But what I didn't say is that I took a whole weekend to write it.** These days, of course, I could do it in 5 or 10 minutes. I don't mean to brag, I just want to point out that skill comes through experience. Eventually, as you get into the rhythm of the business, you'll have done it so many times that you know, instinctively, what needs to be in there. **All you have to do is change the content relating to whatever product you're trying to sell.**

At the time I didn't know that, but what I did know was that I had a big collection of old moneymaking magazines that I found impossible, even back then, to throw away. So I sifted and sorted through a bunch of the ads that I liked the most. We had a theme in mind and we had a little book we were selling for $12.95. **I spent the whole weekend just studying the elements of different ads**

until I found one that I modeled ours after very closely. That got us a good start. It was so exciting in the beginning; we were like two kids in a candy store. After having been in a local business for a few years, it was so thrilling to get cash, checks, and money orders from all over the country, from people we didn't know and would probably never meet.

Building the Business

As I've mentioned previously, during that first six months or so, we created a nice revenue of $16,000 a month with our small advertisements -- and then we met Russ von Hoelscher and made the jump to real success. Russ had already been in the market for decades by then -- he's probably one of the top three most knowledgeable people I know in this field -- and he happened to see our ads. He sent for our initial booklet, liked what he saw, and sent us a brochure on his consulting services. He included a little personal note saying, "Hey I've seen your stuff, I like what you're doing, I think I can help you," and told us to give him a call. **Well, thank God I did give him a call because it changed our lives.** The first thing that Russ did was to encourage us to start running full-page ads. I wrote the ads myself; Russ wrote the headlines.

I'll never forget when Russ asked me later down the road, "Why didn't you just let me write the ad for you?" Quite simply, there was something in me then that wanted to do it myself. **I didn't want to just hire it out, this was a skill that I wanted to learn, something that really interested me. The whole idea that you could put words on a piece of paper and people would send you money -- well, that was wild.** I didn't want to just abdicate that to somebody else; I wanted to do it. So I wrote that myself and, again, it took me an awful long time to do it. Russ wrote the headline, though, and that headline was responsible for a great deal of the success of that ad.

It was a brilliant headline. It led people into the body copy. I'm looking at it right now, I've got it right here on my wall. It says "$825 a day receiving phone calls" on the first line. And then, on the bottom line, it says in a reverse type, "And you never have to talk to anyone." Then there's a picture of my wife and I. That was the headline for our Dialing for Dollars book, the one we ran for four years. That's the book that took us from $300 to $10 million. It was a good book, we sold about 150,000 copies. **But more importantly than that, we had all kinds of back-end stuff that we sold to the customers afterward.** We developed customers we still have to this day, people who are still with us, still spending money. Those back-end sales form another vitally important part of this business, one I'll discuss in detail later in the book.

For now, just let me say this: we have a lot of customers who have spent tens of thousands of dollars with us. That's one form of proof that this is a marketplace that can truly make you rich. **If you'll just do some of the things I'm going to tell you to do in this book, you can develop your own set of customers who will end up giving you thousands and thousands of dollars.** Again, you just have to do a few things right. You have to immerse yourself in the marketplace by sending away for everything, by looking for the common denominators, and by considering carefully all of the secrets I'm going to reveal to you here. You have to create your own money-making program or you have to be part of somebody else's book that gives you a super-high profit margin.

You can't work on just 50% or, in most cases, 60%. **You have to have more money than that, because your costs can be high, especially in the new-customer-acquisition department.** You have to build the trust of these people and that's very easy to do if you treat them right -- because there are so many crooks out there in the marketplace.

There are a lot of others who, if they're not crooks, are

"fly-by-nighters." They're people who have no real knowledge of the long-term nature of this business, they're in it for a quick buck, and they really don't know what they're doing. They're "hit and run." **They make a lot of money in the short run, but they don't value the relationship with the customer, so they have really no back end.**

And that's really very stupid. **They don't realize that that's where all the profit is in this business -- it's on the back end, the long-term relationships.** They're very short-sighted by nature and the marketplace is filled with these people. One of the reasons why a lot of people are turned off by the opportunity market is because they see all these people in it. There are literally thousands of people out there -- probably tens of thousands -- running various ads and websites touting a wide variety of products and services that supposedly show people how to make more money. Yet most of those people don't understand many of the things I'm going to talk about in this book. They're making lots of mistakes and they're not getting even a small fraction of the money that they could and should be getting.

First and foremost, you need to have something that has value. **In other words, somebody has to be able to actually do something and see the results because, if you sell something that doesn't work, they're never going to come back and buy anything from you again.** Years ago, when we were selling our Dialing for Dollars book, we had people who were making tens of thousands of dollars every single month. We had one guy in Salt Lake City, Provo area, J. Peterson, who was doing over $5 million every year and that was back when we were doing just a couple of million a year! He was selling our books and I know he was making that money because he was coming back through us. He was placing these huge wholesale orders to get some of the stuff that he was selling. We had plenty of other people who were also placing huge wholesale orders with us.

So, what would happen is we'd go to the mailbox, and everyday we'd pull out these letters from people saying, "Oh man! We love you guys, you're helping us make so much money, and we've never made this much money in our entire lives." And you'd be feeling good about yourself -- then you'd open up another letter and it would say, "You scumbags! You're cheating me and I'm going to turn you into the Better Business Bureau." Or, "I'm going to turn you into the FTC." "I'm going to turn you into the US Postal Inspectors," "I'm going to call my attorney general." **And it really tore us to pieces, so we decided to try to figure out what was it that was causing some of these people to make tens of thousands a month with the same exact book, while other people were going broke.** The only common denominator we found was that all of our successful distributors had had some kind of previous business experience before they purchased our book, whereas all the people that were unsuccessful had very little, or none.

So, why does that make such a difference? Because, I think, people with no real business experience just quit way too soon. I've discovered that many of the people who never make money always think they're smarter than they are, they think they're smarter than the person they bought the information from, or think they're smarter than the person they're working with to grow their business. **Of course, I think that in order to be an entrepreneur, part of what it takes in the beginning is a sense of rebelliousness: that rebellious side of them that says, "Screw this! I'm never going to make anybody else rich ever again.** I'm going to go on my own. I'm going to do my own thing. I'm going to call my own shots. I'm going to be free. I'm better and smarter than my boss." I think some of that's good in the beginning, in terms of trying to get started.

But, I also know that very quickly into the game, that same entrepreneur had better start recognizing all the things that they're weak at and come face-to-face with their inadequacies, so that they

---

can go ahead and assemble a team of other people who have the knowledge, skills, and abilities that they don't. If they don't do that, they'll fail. That's all there is to it. The same is true if you fail to pay attention to what the people who've gone before you have to say. **Being a maverick is all well and good, but if you buy a book on marketing and you think to yourself, "I'm smarter than this," or "I can shortcut this; I don't need to do this," or "This is unimportant -- this I never will do because it's just not my style," then you're sabotaging yourself.** You're throwing away a process that's been proven many, many times. You're not only failing to learn, but you're failing to put money in your pocket.

Sure, sometimes there's a big learning curve involved. Some of the things I'm going to talk about in this book, things that are very matter-of-fact from my perspective, came from a lot of pain and struggle due to a serious initial learning curve that had to be experienced if I was going to profit at all.

My best story about that occurred in 1994 when Dan Kennedy produced an infomercial for us. (I wrote all the sales copy.) Our infomercial resulted in a bunch of leads coming in—we were selling a $3,000 business opportunity —but I just wasn't able to convert enough sales to make a profit because of the high cost of the infomercial. **I kept telling Dan how I was working my ass off, how I was doing this and that, and he kept saying, "You're giving up on them too quick."** <u>What he meant was, we weren't following up on the back end enough</u>. I got so irritated with him -- but I realize now that there's a lot I had to learn about follow-ups with customers. **Now, thanks to that painful lesson and the skills that we've developed since, it's not uncommon at all for us to send as many as 14--20 different follow-ups out to a lead that we can't convert with an initial sale before we finally give up on them.**

Now, by doing that infomercial, we potentially lost millions of dollars that we could have gotten otherwise -- but you never know about things like that. It was definitely a painful, costly lesson. And since then, yes, we've had other painful experiences where we lost money. But we've also developed ways to make sure that you never lose any money -- but I'll save that secret for later.

The Direct Mail Era

To go back to my Russ von Hoelscher story: to get us from $16,000 a month to almost $100,000 in sales a week in the first nine months, he got us started in full-page ads. We went from running tiny display ads to running large full-page ads in as many as 10-12 different publications at a time. And then he got us involved in direct mail. **After that, we started making millions of dollars a year and we've never turned back.** In our best year so far, we did almost $15 million in sales. I think that's pretty damned good for a little company in the middle of Kansas with no more than 30-40 employees.

Our first direct-mail opportunity was the same one we started out with: our Dialing for Dollars book. We ran it from 1988 to 1992, until we just couldn't run it anymore; eventually, for whatever reason, it sizzled out. At that point, we had to get on a fresh horse and keep moving forward.

Direct mail was a godsend for us. It let us reach so many more people, in a more direct way, than any display ad ever could. Now, it's an expensive medium -- there's no question about that. When you look at the money that it costs to send a direct mail letter to one specific prospect, you'll see that it's the highest cost of any other medium you can use to reach a particular person. And yet, if you play your cards right and master the process, it can make you an insane amount of money, more than any other form of advertising.

It frustrates me to see marketers who try to spend as little money as they can, in order to make as much money as they can. Sure, I agree with them on one level: you want to be conservative rather than wasteful and certainly you don't want to do anything wild and crazy. Direct mail is expensive. **But you can avoid the worst problems by trying all kinds of different things and testing them to small groups**. If you lose money during a test, you're only losing that little bit you used to test with, so it's really not that risky. Even though you'll spend more on each customer than with other means of advertising, you have the potential to convert more people, and you'll make a lot more money in the long run. That's one key to that phenomenal growth that we've had at M.O.R.E., Inc. The millions and millions of dollars we've made have come to us through direct mail more than anything else.

We also have our own special style that I believe has contributed greatly to our success. Some of our competitors wait until the quarterly counts come up for the mailing lists that they use and then they go ahead and try to get their mail into the people's mailboxes before everybody else and try to profit by getting new customers. There are many, many people in our market who are playing that game. But that's never really been a good idea, in our opinion, because we're in it for the long haul. **Our profits all come from the back end -- and so rather than mailing out 750,000 pieces in one shot, every quarter, we instead chose to send a consistent amount of direct mail on a weekly basis as part of our new customer acquisition program**. Sure, we're not always getting in the mailbox before these other people, but I'm not sure that that's really an important thing, especially since our strategy is based on what our customers do after their first purchases.

Since the early 1990s we've sent out thousands of pieces of mail every single week. **That helps us bring new customers into the fold a few at a time, so we continue to do more and more**

business with them. I believe we were up to 125,000 pieces a week at one point in the early 1990s; that's the most we've ever done. Occasionally since, we've done as many as 75,000-100,000 a week -- but for the past half-decade we've stuck at 50,000 pieces a week for new customer acquisitions. And these aren't postcards -- for the most part, they're larger direct mail packages. They bring in a steady stream of new customers.

We only stop for a couple of weeks around Christmas -- and the last couple of years, we haven't even done that. Until we experimented with it, we always just assumed you have to stop mailing around Christmas time. **But now we're mailing during the Christmas season and I guarantee that ours will be just about the only direct mail packages in people's mailboxes at that time of year because nobody mails around Christmas time.** The theory is that everyone is going to be so focused on the holiday they're not going to pay attention to what you're doing.

You need to try things like this, to see what comes of them. **Just let the numbers tell you what to do.** <u>Test everything you can think of and follow the numbers.</u> The marketing plan we've used to make so many millions of dollars is so simple it's not even funny. We've got a regular campaign out there always, every single day of every single week, to bring in a steady flow of new customers -- and then we've got all kinds of ways to segment our customer base so that we can communicate to different groups of customers in different ways. We do this so we know who our very best customers are, so we can take better care of them and create specific offers for them that nobody else is doing. And then, through a series of back-end promotions, we're continually trying to re-sell to our established customers as many times as we can. We keep our printers constantly busy -- during any particular period, up to 80% percent of the stuff they're printing is ours. **We're constantly, consistently sending things out every single week -- so our customer list is being bombarded with new**

information, new products, new opportunities, and it's a consistent relationship building process.

People look at our stuff and they really don't understand our success. **But it's simple: a small part of it is persistence and, yes, maybe talent -- but 90% is just an intimate knowledge of the marketplace, based on realizing that this is the world's largest niche market, as I love to say.** Even though there are millions of people out there who habitually buy various moneymaking plans and books, they're basically like a small niche market -- meaning that they all have the same behavior. **They have the same psychographics: they think alike.** Once you get a feel for that, you develop a lot of confidence and, once you can break through their skepticism, you can build long-term relationships with them -- and that's where you make money.

You have to be careful, though. Don't overwhelm them. Once, fairly recently, I did get a little over-aggressive -- and I got into some financial trouble because of it. It's going to be a long time before I ever do that again, if ever. **You see, if you know your market well, it's generally safe to spend a significant amount of money on acquiring each new customer because you'll earn that money and more back over the lifetime of the relationship.** Well, this time we were spending up to $500 for every new customer that was just coming aboard at less than $50. That sounds pretty backward, but we then started selling them back-end products and we were able to make a nice profit -- before I stretched it a little too thin and got myself into some deep financial difficulties because I was too aggressive.

When my wife ran the company, she was very conservative. She always insisted that we break even on the front end, meaning that if we sold a $30 product, there had to be enough sales that came in off that initial promotion to cover the cost of the direct mail space advertising we were using.

But I knew that the people who made the most money in direct response marketing were huge, Fortune 1000 companies that don't care so much about initial costs. They make huge amounts of money through direct marketing -- up to hundreds of millions a year -- and they simply don't think that way. **They look at the expense that it takes to acquire a new customer as an investment towards future profits.** They don't necessarily try to focus that much on how much money it cost to bring them in, but on how fast they can make all the money back -- how long it takes to fill that gap between initial costs and profits.

Now, this is a worthwhile strategy, assuming you can afford it -- though I didn't have deep enough pockets to keep playing that game. **But let me re-emphasize that a lot of the people in this marketplace who <u>never</u> get rich are people who don't realize the real value of re-selling these same customers over and over again <u>because they will keep buying</u> -- as long as they know you're really developing good, solid programs and are focused on customer service.** By that, I mean that you're dedicated on trying to deliver the best programs you can, products that will stand the greatest chance of making your customers the most money in the quickest time. As long as people feel that your heart's in the right place, you've got good, strong money-bank guarantees, and you're making them good offers that they can't say no to, they will buy and re-buy from you indefinitely. **You're there to produce a product that's going to allow somebody else to learn more and to get themselves up higher on the learning curve so they can go out and create more money.** That's the essence of a moneymaking opportunity; it's so simple. Dan Kennedy jokes that I want to turn everything into a business opportunity. I've thought about that and the truth is that almost anything can be turned into a business opportunity.

It starts with a product or service that's for sale, that's Number One. Number Two is that you need a marketing plan to

---

sell it with. Number Three, you need to provide all the turnkey materials. You need to combine all of that into a package that people can buy. That gives them the products and services to sell and things that they really feel good about. **There has to be a continual commitment -- just like with a good network marketing program.**

Join a good multi-level marketing program and you'll see a great business opportunity in action. **They have great products, they give you the marketing plans, they give you a little motivation to go out there and make money with it, and then they package it all together so that it's as effortless and confusion-free as it can possibly be.** With this kind of program, you show people what they have to do to go out there and sell the product or service.

Of course, the business opportunities that sell the best are the ones that promise the most money potential on every transaction or that offer some residual income of some type on the back end. Later on in this book, I'll share some ways to make that happen. It's really simple -- there's nothing complicated about it. People are looking for something that sounds new or different or exciting, so you've got to find some hook or angle to wrap your whole business opportunity around. <u>The better you can combine those elements, the easier it becomes</u>. This is, a course, a function of experience, but as I mentioned earlier, that's easy to acquire. You have to go out there and purposely try to get on as many mailing lists as you possibly can. You send away for opportunity after opportunity and, pretty soon, your name is going to be traded back and forth between all of these different opportunity sellers and you're going to end up on everybody's mailing list.

Every day when you open your mailbox, it's going to be stuffed full. You're going to learn through osmosis, to a degree, just by simply being a good customer and deciding that you're going to buy a bunch of the stuff and by trying to look at it from a business person's standpoint rather than a consumer's standpoint.

Chapter Two

The List of Seven

In this chapter I'll discuss the seven strategies that you need to use in order to get super rich. I could probably spend a whole chapter -- or even a whole book -- on each one, but I'll try to contain myself here!

Step One

The first step is actually the most important of all seven and I've already discussed it a great deal here: **Develop an affinity with your marketplace. There's a tremendous amount of power in that, no matter what your marketplace may be.** If you study the lives of the people that have made the most money in your marketplace, you'll find that all of them -- all of them -- have an intimate knowledge of the marketplace that they're serving. If you want to get rich in the opportunity market, nothing's more important than having a real, intimate feeling for who these millions of people you're marketing to are. These are people in pain; these are people who are confused and frustrated. A lot of them are very angry; they feel lied to, cheated, and misled. They've got a right to feel that way. They've tried a lot of different things, so they're constantly in an emotional turmoil.

One of the reasons the opportunity market is such a lucrative marketplace is simply because of this massive pain that these people are under. So what you have to do is speak to their pain, speak to their frustration -- and remember, you need to realize just how skeptical they are. You can't pussyfoot around with that particular aspect of their pain. You have to address their skepticism head on; you have to let them know that you don't blame them for being skeptical. **The marketers who do the best job at letting the customers know that they're understood are the ones who make the most money.** This was very easy for Eileen and I because we were those people.

For years, we sent away for every plan and program we could get our hands on. We were in great pain, we struggled, we were angry, we were skeptical, we were confused; in short, we were going through all that emotional trauma ourselves so, when it came to developing specific offers for products and services for this market, it was easy for us. **We understood the customer and were able to communicate in a direct, forceful, clear, and compelling way.** <u>If you don't have that experience, you need to get it</u>. Nothing takes the place of people feeling like they're understood -- and you have to really understand what drives this marketplace. It's emotional pain.

Step into your customers' shoes and feel that pain. There's no experience like direct experience. **Sure, you can get it in other ways, but that intimate knowledge, that key force in creating millions of dollars in the opportunity marketplace, lies in understanding the fact that the people that you're communicating to are in great emotional pain.** We try to encourage all of our best clients to get into the opportunity market themselves, because, first, there are just too many scam artists in this business who are lying and cheating and stealing for a living. We need more ethical, honest people who have integrity in the field. **Second it takes one to know one -- it's the people who have suffered who can do the best job serving their clients.** Our clients need to take that knowledge, turn it around, and get on the other side of the cash register -- so they can start thinking more like a businessperson than consumers.

You can get a feeling for the total confusion in this

marketplace simply by reading the opportunity magazines out there and by looking at all the different business opportunities up for sale. The Internet just makes it even worse. **You've got information overload: everybody and their brother is claiming they can help you make millions of dollars.** You just don't know who to trust -- and then you get ripped off and you get cheated. There are many, many companies out there whose "proven moneymaking plans" are more fiction than anything.

You and I both know that there are also lots of people out there who have found a formula for creating revenue and the products that they're selling are old. The strategies are old, the behavior they're expecting their customers to perform with is old -- but because people still buy into that sizzle, they're able to sell that same old crap to new people, month in and month out, sometimes for decades. **The promises and the hype are all around and it's almost impossible to tell a good opportunity from a bogus one.** That's one of the reasons you need to develop a list of customers who like you, who trust you, and who believe in you -- people who know that if they're not happy, they're going to get their money back. **Those people are far more inclined to continue to do business with you, even if some of the products they purchased from you haven't given them exactly what they wanted.** They realize that the hope is still alive and they know you're going to take good care of them -- <u>and that's a key to developing the back-end business</u>. It's essential for the millions of dollars in profit that you, as my reader, clearly want to earn. That's the first step, nothing can replace it. It's simply the most important part of the equation.

To put it bluntly, you have to develop an affinity for your market, a genuine understanding and liking for the people you serve. **When you have that, it's easy to sit down and work for hours or days to create great products and services for them.** These people are your good friends. You have a connection with them, an emotional bond where they feel you understand them and

---

CHAPTER TWO

CHAPTER TWO 31

you feel that they understand you. It's a deeper level of understanding of who that person is and what they're all about, what turns them on, what turns them off, what their pains and problems are, what their biggest challenges, their hopes, fears, and dreams are. These are the things you have to really get a good sense for before you can ever really earn the kind of money you could be making.

Step Two

I've already alluded to Step Two here. Even if you don't have a complete, working affinity with your market, you've got to take Step Two anyway. **You need to familiarize yourself with every single business opportunity you can**. Send off for every bit of free information, special reports, and marketing offers you can. Study your market. Go get a copy of Popular Mechanics. Send away for a couple of hundred there. Grab a USA Today weekend edition, call all the biz-op numbers, and send away for everything. Go to websites, sign up, and request all kinds of information. **What's going to happen is this: before long, your name's going to end up on every single mailing list in the business and your mailbox is going to be jam-packed with different moneymaking opportunities of every kind.**

What this is going to do is let you immerse yourself in the marketplace. If you don't have an affinity for the market, if you've never been an opportunity seeker yourself, someone who's gone out there and has these emotional ties I talked about in Step One -- well, this is going to help you get a feel for the marketplace. It'll let you find the common denominators in your market. **You should create a huge swipe file where you keep all the best literature that you receive and start looking at all the sales material not through the eyes of a consumer but as an entrepreneur.** Get on the other side of the cash register and start thinking like a person who wants to make millions in this market and you'll see there's a lot of crap out there.

Another recommendation along this line is to find the ten companies in this marketplace that are making a ton of money and study their stuff alone. But I think it's better to just get as much stuff as you possibly can so you can categorize it, see what works, and put aside all the best material. **By immersing yourself in everything out there, you'll realize there are millions of people who are hungry for this kind of information.** They're sending away for the same stuff you're sending away for and you'll soon see that there's so much confusion in this market -- because everybody's promising all kinds of great things. **If you're a customer in this marketplace and you're really searching for a way to make money, you're basically trying to find a needle in a haystack, those few companies that have something really cool, really good, really solid, and really proven.** It's frustrating because everybody wants to make their opportunity sound like it's the best thing since sliced bread and that's where a lot of this confusion comes from. When customers do invest in these opportunities, many of them fail to deliver half of what was promised to them in the sales material; that makes it even more frustrating.

Send away for this material, study it closely, and you'll get a sense of the frustration and confusion in the marketplace. But you'll also see certain common denominators that appear in almost everybody's sales material. **There are certain triggers, things that the most successful people in our business used over and over again to try to get interest and attention and cause people to invest in our different opportunities.** Look at a hundred different sales letters and soon you'll start seeing common denominators -- and that's a strength. Once you can identify what those things are, you have the power to reproduce them and create your own business opportunities.

When you get right down to it, this is something like going back to school -- doing the research, finding out what works, and what doesn't. **School is never out for people who are committed to making the most amount of money they can.** It's an education thing, but it doesn't have to be terribly taxing. You might be on the couch watching TV with a bowl of popcorn next to you, with a shoebox full of sales letters and packages that came in that day. While you're relaxing, you can flip through them and take notes about the things you find. It's still studying and, what happens is that after a while, it becomes second nature to you. <u>You get a real feel for the marketplace and you start seeing certain themes that reappear over and over again.</u> **There's a language to this marketplace that the most successful people who are knocking down the most money understand intimately.** You'll begin to understand it, after you subject yourself to all these different ads for a while -- plus you'll get a feel for what's out there and who's doing it.

I think it's safe to say that there are successful people in every marketing niche and every genre. If you just look at what they do and emulate them -- not copy them -- then that's a lot of work you don't have to do. You don't need to reinvent the wheel. This process is a real shortcut and that's why we always recommend keeping swipe files and finding the time to work on and go through them on a regular basis. All the ideas that you're looking for to make huge sums of money with are out there now. **Other people are using these ideas; all you have to do is collect them and be smart enough to put them into action when developing your own materials.** Don't copy them outright, but start taking a little bit from here, a little bit from there, and patchwork quilt it all together to create your own unique opportunity that can potentially make you millions of dollars. So, yes, this is homework -- homework that can make you rich.

I like what my good friend Dan Kennedy has to say on the

subject: "Rich and successful people have huge libraries; poor people have huge TVs." **Those of us who do the best in the marketing field are always learning. We're always growing, always expanding, and in the beginning it's very important to study what other people are doing.** After a while, you don't have to spend so much time with that because you've mastered some of the skills necessary to make the money you want, but in the very beginning, you've got to immerse yourself in this marketplace. It would be foolish to think you could go out there and create some multimillion-dollar deal without the kind of experience that comes from all the studying.

Step Three

Step Three is this: learn what the people in this market want the most and <u>then give them only those things</u>. Not what they need, not what you think they need, not even what you think they want -- but what they really want the most. So what do the people in this market want the most? That's pretty simple, although you'll see a lot of different variations on this theme. **They want turnkey systems.**

Okay, so what's a turnkey system? **It's something that gives the customer everything they need in one box.** It gives them the products to sell, it gives them the sales material to sell those products with, and it gives them a start-up manual that shows them how to use this sales material to sell the product or service. That's pretty much everything. You see, this is a marketplace that wants things that sound very easy.

One of the richest people I've ever met in this market is a man named George Douglas. At the time I met him, in September of 1990, George was making about $3,000,000 a month -- but he's gone on to double that. I got to spend a little

---

bit of time with George and the most important thing he told me was this: **"The key to making money in this business is that it's got to sound good."**

Now, some people would say that that's deceptive or misleading, but the truth is that you've got a lot of competition out there who are trying to get the same money that you're trying to get so you'd better make your opportunity sound as good as you can. **Don't lie about it.** Don't make statements you can't back up. But make it sound as easy as possible and make it sound new. People in this market also like the new -- they're really in love with the new technology, especially the Internet.

So it's got to sound new, even if there's really nothing new under the sun, as the Book of Ecclesiastes tells us. People love things that seem new. They also love to be first -- so they like VIP positions, they like exclusive distributorship opportunities, and high level gold and platinum level programs. At the same time (and, yes, I know this is just a little contradictory), they want things that are proven and tested.

A good friend of mine, Ken Peterson, is currently promoting a product called Miracle Relief Cream. He got it from another friend of mine and created some special ads and sales letters for it. Then he went out and tested those effectively -- so he proved that the ads and sales letters really sold this Miracle Relief Cream. **Then he just simply packaged it all up into one program and now gives all of his distributors the sales material that he's created, the product, and a little start-up manual.** That's as easy as it get for a business opportunity. What else do people in this market love? Residual income -- the chance to do something one time and get paid forever.

Your best bet for developing an understanding of these business opportunities is to become a client or customer for one of the bigger companies in the marketplace and see what they're doing. Get on their customer list and buy some of their turnkey business opportunities and systems, then emulate accordingly. Alternately, you can become a joint owner or licensee of some company that's already developed materials that they've already tested and proven. **You have to know that your product has value.** It can't just sound good; you can't make all kinds of unfounded claims or that'll blow up in your face. But if it doesn't sound good, if it doesn't sound real, if it doesn't sound immediately valuable, if it doesn't sound interesting, they're never going to go beyond and read the letter and eventually want to buy the product.

More specifically than that, it's got to have some kind of catch to it. There's got to be a hook or an angle; you have to theme the whole thing around some simple concept that's brand new and revolutionary. **It's got to get their attention, but it's got to be simple and something that they can see themselves doing**. That's one of the things that Dan Kennedy taught us very early on. The easier and more simplistic you can make it, the more people are going to respond. The more complicated it sounds, the fewer people will go for it.

Years ago, when we had our first expensive seminar, Russ von Hoelscher and Eileen and I were upstairs talking strategy and Russ said, "Look, let's not tell people that they can make millions real fast, or anything like that. Let's just try to bring them up to speed; let's talk to them about making $50,000 a year first, then double that the next year, and double it again the third."

We all decided that that was the most common sense thing to do, since we didn't want to mislead anybody. So Russ went downstairs and opened up the seminar. We had a couple of hundred people in the room, and he said, "How many people in this room would just like to make an extra $50,000 next year?" He was expecting half the hands to go up -- but not a single one did. So

Russ quickly asked, "All right, how many people want to make millions of dollars?" and all the hands went up -- and some people jumped up and started yelling! Like it or not, accept it or not, that's how our market is. **I'm not saying that it's good or bad, but the people in the opportunity market want to get rich -- really, truly rich -- and they want to do it overnight.** That's the thing that excites them the most. It's just like around the time when the lottery is starting to build and you've got $160 million in there -- and all of a sudden there are long lines forming as people try to get lottery tickets.

The people in this marketplace are looking for a quick buck -- and I don't mean to pass judgment. That's just the way it is. **I was the same way, back in the 1980s, when I was sending away for all these moneymaking plans and books; I wanted to make millions and millions of dollars right away.** If somebody would have told me back then that it was going to take a hell of a lot of work and time and effort, that I was going to have to develop new skills and knowledge and alliances and I was going to have to work my ass off -- well, I would have never sent away for a program like that. There's some insanity in this marketplace; I know that. I'm still an opportunity junkie myself; I'm still sending away for a lot of books, though now it's mostly for research.

But here's something you need to realize about this marketplace. Nothing comes free. **If you really want to get rich, you're going to have to accept the fact that you have to work for it.** Sure, there are secrets that can help you make huge amounts of money -- but it's not going to come by magic. I tell you this not just because it's against the law to tell you otherwise -- and it is -- but because it's true. **I can't promise people they're going to wake up and become an overnight millionaire by doing nothing.** Sure, you always imply that it's possible, that at any given moment, anything can happen and they really could make a lot of money -- because that's part of what really excites people.

I'm just telling you the brutal facts here and I hope you can appreciate it.

Why? Because I think honesty is something that too often gets overlooked in this business. **There's an old saying: "If it sounds too good to be true, it probably is," but people in the opportunity market often put that aside.** One reason is that if you use that same judgmental device on everything that's ever presented to you, you're going to miss out on potentially hundreds of opportunities throughout your lifetime. There are plenty of things that come along that sound too good to be true -- but they're not, if only because of where you are on the learning curve.

The only way I know how to get rich is to get rich quick. I don't believe in getting rich slowly; I think it's boring. I've read all the books on how to become financially independent, but I have no interest in saving small amounts of money so that thirty years later I'll have over a million bucks under my mattress. **The only way that all the wealthy people I admire in this world have made their millions has been quickly, if not overnight; so whoever said there's no such thing as getting rich quick is wrong.**

It can happen, it's just very rare. Just keep in mind the fact that there's a real emotional delusion that a lot of the people in this market have, that it's sure to happen to them -- and I had it too, back in the late 1980s, when I wanted to be a millionaire yet didn't have a pot to pee in. I didn't have any specialized knowledge or skills or abilities. I wasn't blessed with a high IQ -- and yet I wanted to make multi-millions of dollars. I was delusional and I honestly feel that our marketplace is made up of millions of people that share in that delusion, like it or not. **If you don't like it, then don't get involved in the marketplace because that's the large part of what this market is.** Yet, at the same time they're skeptical, so you want to make your program sound good and offer lots of guarantees. You have to make things as risk-free as possible for them and you have to address their skepticism by identifying with it.

People really do want things that sound too good to be true. Remember that movie "A Few Good Men," where Jack Nicholson says, "You can't handle the truth!"? Well, by and large, the people in this marketplace can't handle the truth. **The truth is that if you want to get rich, you're going to have to pay the price.** Yes, we're living in the greatest country on Earth, where anyone can make it to the big time; but to get there, you're going to go through a tremendous learning curve. You're going to have to sacrifice. **You're not just going to wake, go to sleep, wake up the next morning and be worth millions of dollars.** You can't wave a magic wand -- but what you can do is put a little magic to work here and there, and it all adds up. You got to be willing to pay the price through practicing these seven steps.

Step Four

Step Four ties in closely to what I've already been saying. You can get started in this business with a very, very small mission. The secret to getting rich is actually thinking smaller, not bigger! You have to build your foundation with small classified or display ads. I know that that sounds boring and, yes, it is, especially when you compare it to all the high technology that's available out there. But here's the truth. **Maybe people don't want to accept it, and I'm not saying that there are no exceptions to the rule, but for the most part, all that Internet marketing stuff is far too complicated for the beginner.** If you don't have any experience with the business already, you'll be far better off if you start with small ads in popular publications. There are magazines and newspapers out there that are just filled with all kinds of opportunity ads. **If you run a small ad in those magazines you'll never lose money -- you'll always double or triple your money, at worst.** No, you're never going to get rich -- there's not enough of a market for those ads to make you rich -- but if you start with them, you'll develop your confidence a little.

The bad part about these ads is that it takes 4-6 weeks, and in some cases longer, to get your ad placed. But they let you get your feet wet and start making money right away once they come out. Let me repeat: you can't lose with these advertisements, as long as you're using two-step marketing. **First you get people to raise their hands so you can build your list, then you start offering them more products on the back end.** We did that; then we moved on to full page ads and other media like card-decks and then we got into direct mail, which is the real secret to making millions of dollars in this business. Recall, though, that direct mail is also the most expensive medium -- and if you don't know what you're doing and you don't have a proven plan, you're going to lose all your money right away with it.

If you do start small, you're going to make your money and you're going to get some much-needed experience. **As you build your experience, your confidence level is going to grow and then you'll be ready to take on bigger and better things.** But we see so many people who get started and want to go directly into direct mail. This is fine if you're using a proven, tested campaign, but if you're just starting from scratch, it's the wrong thing to do. They lose their money, then they lose their confidence, and the whole thing eventually dies. They never get off to a good start, so they actually end up ruining it for themselves. They're thinking big; well, that's great! You want to be ambitious, fine; hell, I'm ambitious. I want to make millions of dollars; I always have. But they're jumping into the lake at the wrong point.

They should start small, even though that's not very attractive. I understand that there's nothing exciting about running small classified ads. It's the most boring thing you can possibly do in our business. **There's no momentum; you don't see anything**

---

happening until somebody starts sending you money or starts asking for information. Then that nasty gap of 4-6 weeks, in some cases up to 12 weeks, while you're waiting for your ad to come out. When compared to all the high tech fancy advertising with its bells and whistles and hype -- well, that makes it look even worse!

But I'm here to tell you there's no better way to get the biggest bang for your buck. You don't have to stick to the popular opportunity magazines, either; take a look at the backs of magazines like Popular Mechanics, Popular Science, and a host of others. They've got strong classified ad sections where other business opportunity sellers advertise constantly. Go to the biggest bookstore in your area and look through all the magazines (if they'll let you). **Find out where all the other business opportunity people are advertising, that's where you want to be.** It's just like if you had a fast food joint; what's the one restaurant you want to be right next to? McDonald's, right? Well, it's the same way in this business. **Find out where all the biz-op sellers are advertizing, that's where you should put your ads.** Follow the leaders, at least at first; let other people be the guinea pigs.

Then, work from the middle of the circle toward the outside. Start with the magazines that offer the greatest probability of success for your ads -- the opportunity magazines. If you look at these publications, you'll note that they're mostly just ads anyway; the only people that read them are those are desperately seeking a business opportunity. **To attract them, your advertisement has to be somewhat unique -- that's part of the key here.** Then you go on to other media and experiment with them and, eventually, of course, all paths lead to direct mail, if you really want to make some decent money. This is the medium that can make you super rich. But because of its high cost, if you don't know what you're doing and if you don't have a firm foundation -- which is what Step Four here is all about -- then you're going to lose your ass. You

---

might as well take your money and go to Vegas or take it and flush it down the toilet.

Step Five

Not all customers are created equal, that's our fifth step. You hear popular slogans from businesses about how all their customers are important to them and, yes, at some level that's true. **But when it comes to marketing, to making money, your best customers are always going to be the ones who buy more from you than all the rest do.** Those people are more important than everyone else. It's a fact that 80% of your profits are going to come from 20% of your customers -- though in our business, it's more like 90-10.

What you have to do is segment your customer list, separate out your best customers from the rest. You know that they're more serious than the rest and, chances are, the reason they're spending that money with you is because they have more money to spend. **The secret to getting rich is to continue to get these people to re-buy from you -- so you're looking for people that have money.** Not only do they spend more money with you because they have more money to spend, they've also shown that they trust you -- or they wouldn't keep spending. When somebody sends you their money, they're really voting with their checkbook. It's an act of faith on their part. Faith in you.

When you're developing a new promotion, do so with your very best customers first. Those are the people you present the offer to first. If your best customers won't buy your offer, then none of your customers are going to buy it -- and you're never going to lose money by trying to sell it to your best customers. **The trust is already there. They'll buy anything from you, as long as they know they can get their money back if they're not**

---

happy. If you have your list segmented this way, every time you come up with an idea for a new product or system or program, you can take it straight to your very, very best customers and try to sell it there first.

At the very worst, you're going to break even, so you are never going to have to worry about losing money. Then you take the offers that work best and find a way to expand them though the rest of your customer base. Now you're starting to go outside the middle of the circle. If the offer still produces tremendous profits, then you use those as your opportunities for new customer acquisition -- and now you're going outside the circle with that super-hot offer to people who've never bought anything from you. This is a way that you can limit all your risks. **It isn't gambling; you're taking calculated risks, and it's a great testing ground to find out which of your offers are strong enough to offer to people you don't already have a relationship with, in order to try to bring them into the circle.**

Does it make sense to reward your best customers when you're trying out these various offers? Sure, you have to -- that's part of the way you make your best customers know how much you appreciate them. **You're always coming out with things that are special to them; you're giving them all kinds of VIP offers.** People in this marketplace love pre-publication offers, for example. They want to be the first in line. So you can just come up with some wild and crazy idea for a new promotion and throw it out to your best customers. Tell them that it's not even ready yet, but because it's not ready yet and because they're one of your very best customers and you love them and you want to take good care of them, you're going to give it to them for 50% off the regular price. Just make sure they realize that the product is still in development.

So you get a whole bunch of people saying, "Yes, I want to

be first!" Now they're all sending you their cash, checks, money orders, and credit card authorizations -- and you've got a lot of incentive to work 24/7 to complete the project so you can get it out to them. That's another no-risk strategy you can use with your best customers to not only make sure you never lose any money, but also to inspire yourself. **When you've got a thousand people who have given you a couple of hundred or a couple of thousand dollars each -- well, talk about motivation.**

You know that unless you get it done by the date you said you were going to get it done by, you're going to have a lot of people who want their money back. That's anathema! You want to make sure that you keep the money that's already come in. **Plus, you want to make sure that you don't irritate your best customers.** We all need things to motivate ourselves, especially creative people for whom implementation is always a struggle.

We've always got more projects than we can handle and I can't think of any better way to develop them than to offer them to your best customers and admit to them that you're not done yet. You're not lying to them, even if in many cases you haven't even started the product yet. It's just that you write the sales letter first, which is what you're supposed to do anyway, and then you create the product. **In this case, all you have to do is what you have to do in general with all advertising: you have to deliver on what was promised.** Your best customers already know they can get their money back anytime they're not happy. And as long as you're keeping in touch with them and letting them know the progress of the project or the product, then you're golden.

So, all customers aren't created equal, sadly; those who spend more money with you deserve more, and you can afford to spend more money on them in an attempt to sell to them than you can with the people who aren't your best customers. Once you've got your list segmented and you've got a group of customers who

---

have spent 3-5 times more money with you, on average, than the rest of your customers, you can now afford to spend 3-5 times more money on marketing to them.

The Number One thing you have to be aware of when you start segmenting these customers is that you need to segment them in different ways. First, split them up by the dollar amount they spend; you need to have some way of quantifying that. You can also segment them by the type of product or services they buy from you. In some cases, they can be segmented by the year or the quarter that they start buying from you. These are just some of the ways we segment. We have what we call our Primo A thru D lists -- A and B are the highest -- and the qualifications required to get into each of the segments are all based on dollar amounts. Somebody who spends more money with us moves up to a qualified customer group.

Now, we never segment by age; it's just not applicable to our market. We don't want to know the ages of our customers. That's not important to us. In fact, the idea that it might be is a bit of a sore spot with me. For years, people who really don't understand our business have noted the number of older people at our seminars and have accused us of taking advantage of senior citizens. That really pisses me off, not to put too fine a point on it. We don't know what the ages of our customers are until we meet them face-to-face! The neat thing about the business opportunity market is that it's filled with people of every demographic, old and young -- from teenagers all the way up to octogenarians. **This is a marketplace filled with people of every age bracket and every religious creed and every race and level of education.** We have doctors and lawyers and retired business people who are worth $40-50 million and who are bored out of their minds; they're looking for some opportunity to keep them busy. Then again, we have a lot of up-and-comers, people who are like we once were. **The one thing that connects all the millions of people in this**

market together is the desire to make huge sums of money. They're looking for proven ways to do it; they're looking for easy systems; they want the latest new thing, anything that sounds new and exciting.

We aren't pandering to old people here. In fact, I'm ashamed that we're living in country where older people aren't given the respect they deserve. Yes, we've turned them into victims. Some of them have even bought into that mindset -- and that's wrong. **I respect the older people that we do business with a great deal: they're going for it. They're still excited and they still have lots of life in them. They're looking for something to get excited about.** They're looking for something to recapture the energy and enthusiasm they had when they were younger, when they were involved in their careers, when they were important in this world and they were doing things to contribute. **That's what this business does.** That's what business is all about; it's what making money is all about.

I couldn't live with myself if I were deliberately and cynically targeting retired people. **But I do want to point out that oftentimes when people retire, they've suddenly got lots of time on their hands -- but they're not through living yet.** They're still looking for that special opportunity and this is one of the reasons why the opportunity market is only going to grow and thrive in coming years -- because look at what's happening with the Baby Boomers. It's retirement time for the older members of this cohort and there are more than 70 million of us in America alone! **In another 10-20 years, this marketplace is going to literally explode with growth because, once the baby boomers retire and then go and play golf for six months, they're going to end up bored to tears and ready to get back into the swing of things.** They're going to be looking for opportunities to augment those pensions funds that they're getting because that ain't gonna cut it, baby -- especially if they're depending on Social Security.

Step Six

This is one of my favorites. Now, I love building relationships -- but they usually take so much time. That's why Step Six is so important. **It simply involves making alliances and building quick relationships with other smart marketers, who are living and thriving in the market right now, and who can help you make more money.** I know it may sound selfish, but they say that you're who you hang around with and I believe that. I also believe that you have only so much time and energy -- so my relationships, except for a few personal family ones, are all with people that I'm also in business with. I've taken my business and mixed it with my friendships. **That's the essence of what all joint venturing is supposed to be about: people come together to do business together so the revenue that's generated from that combination is much more that you would ever make on your own.** In some cases, my joint venture partners have cut me checks for millions of dollars. That's money we never would have earned without them and, frankly, they earned a lot they wouldn't have without us. It's a synergistic relationship, in many ways.

In addition, this is a great way of strengthening your knowledge of the marketplace. **Being an entrepreneur in general can be a lonely thing, because you're working ungodly numbers of hours sometimes, and you're working a lot harder than most people will ever work.** Even if, in a sense, it's not really like work because it's your hobby and your passion all rolled into one, you still need that human touch. There's a certain kinship we entrepreneurs have with each other and we need to hang around with more of the type of people who are moving in same direction we're moving in.

One big mistake I see a lot in this field, especially among Internet marketers, is that for some reason they want to isolate themselves; they want to live their whole life **in front of the computer screen. I see too many people who aren't making any effort to build and maintain relationships with other people -- in fact, they're trying to avoid that.**

One of the reasons they're attracted to Internet marketing is so they can shut out that part of their life. The Internet is anonymous. **They're doing the whole Internet thing because they don't have to communicate with anybody, they don't have to talk with anybody** -- and yet the true essence of building a business online is that, sooner or later, some of those people you're avoiding are going to be some of the most important people you communicate with.

Unfortunately, they've never seen that kind of relationship blossom into something that's going to put money into their pocket. **Ultimately, what happens is that these isolationists try to do everything by themselves.** They're way too stubborn and independent and they're way too narrow-minded when it comes to sharing the kind of revenue that a good joint venturer shares with his or her partners.

In our business, the people who can help us make the most money are the ones we must place the most value on. The best joint venture relationships are those in which you continue to find ways to do business with the same people again and again. **As you trust each other more, you're able to come up with ideas together that neither of you would ever have come up with on your own.** There's a knowledge share involved, too. If you learn something, you're not supposed to keep it to yourself. In some way, you're supposed to impart that wisdom to other people. Whether you get any money for it or not, the idea is that you're still supposed to share it. Then you train your friends to do the same for you.

You try to find as many good people as you can, people

who have the talents and abilities that you most admire or you lack within yourself, so that you can create synergistic relationships. You try to take good care of the people who are taking good care of you and, when you do run into an occasional person who's not a long-term player, who is greedy and manipulative, and is going to do nothing but cheat you and rip you off -- well, you get rid of those people as fast as you can.

One of the reasons we've continued to do business with the same people year after year is that it's easy. **Once you trust somebody and build up a certain amount of respect and friendship, why would you not want continue to find as many ways as possible to keep working with them?** Once you've shared success with someone, it's only natural for you to sit down and say, "Okay, now what else can we do?" And you know what? There's always something that you can do next because part of the secret to getting rich in the opportunity market is that you're living in the world of intangible now. **The business is only limited by your imagination**. When you put a couple people together who have an intimate knowledge of the marketplace -- or better still, you put four or five people together -- the ideas are going to continue to get better and better.

All it takes is one good business opportunity to make you millions of dollars. So it helps to have people that you can call on, who have done what you want to do, who have gone where you want to go, who have the experience and are interested in the same types of thing. Their knowledge becomes yours and vice versa. It's a synergistic relationship, as I mentioned earlier. The sum total is greater than the individual parts; what you create ends up being far greater than you could ever have done on your own.

Jim Rohn, the famous motivational success coach, teaches people that if you want to get rich, all you have to do is take a millionaire out for lunch. Admittedly, that's not so easy to do -- but it's a fact that most successful people want to share their experiences with others. Even if they're overworked and overscheduled, their hearts tend to be in the right place. They really do want to help you -- and of course a lot of them are doing seminars and workshops and they produce a ton of different books and programs sharing their greatest ideas. Part of that's because they want to make money, of course -- I won't lie to you about that! **But part of it's also because they have a strong desire to extend a hand to up-and-coming people who are just getting started.**

You have to realize that successful entrepreneurs can recognize that ambition in the new folks because we all had it in the beginning, too. When we meet somebody who's just getting started, who has the same look in their eyes that we had at one point, it just makes us want to reach out and extend our hand to them.

That's what Russ Von Hoelscher did to us when we first got started; he became our Dutch uncle. And because he's just a little bit older than us and had already been in the business for twenty years when he met us he took us under his wing and really worked with us. Of course, he was trying to make money -- and we did end up paying him many thousands of dollars. **But he also did it from a genuine desire on his part to help a couple of kids who were just as ambitious and hungry as he'd once been.** I just see so many seasoned veteran entrepreneurs who have the same desire, people who really want to help lift other people up.

I think Russ also knew the value that these relationships could bring to him further down the road. Russ is a very sharp guy and -- whoever said money and friendship don't mix -- well, those people never met him. Now, when you take a pre-existing friendship and try to build a business around it, that becomes a recipe for disaster more times than not. **But when you start a brand new relationship with somebody in the same business you're in, and you find out that they're a good person and they**

find out same about you and you do some business where you all make money together, it becomes fun. It really does become the essence of what all friendship is supposed to be and, in some ways, it's actually even better than most relationships because most relationships aren't as cut-and-dried as a business relationship can be.

In a good business relationship, you love your friends and they love you, but they're also trying to help you make money and you're doing the same for them. So it's clearer and more focused, whereas a relationship that's not based on business may not be so clear or focused.

I do know, through all the different alliances that we've built over the years, we've learned a lot of things that we never would have otherwise. Those six years that we were involved with Dan Kennedy's Platinum Group were essential to my growth as a marketer -- and there are plenty of other relationships out there, just waiting for you to get involved with. **You can join forces with people who are moving on the same path that you are and my advice is: find people who are super-talented and super-smart.** Latch onto them and don't let them go.

It's pretty simple, really, it sounds like basic common sense. But I run into so many entrepreneurs who lack people skills. They're way too independent, stubborn, or greedy for their own good. They're trying to get as much as they can on every deal, rather than looking at the long term -- and they're very difficult to work with. So my advice is to be a lot less insular than you might otherwise be. Try joint ventures, but don't try to be greedy. Follow the golden rule. **You're not out there to take every dollar that comes in; you need to be flexible with your partners.** You need to give and take, to be liberal and fair. Get this right and it'll bring in huge amounts of money over the long term.

Step Seven

Step Seven is planning and organizing. At M.O.R.E., Inc., we have regular weekly meetings with a staff of people who have been with us for years, people who really understand our business. We number all of our mailings and we're constantly scheduling new promotions. Our printer is always there at each meeting. Our mailing house is always there, too, as are the key staff members who make these mailings and these promotions happen. We've been doing it like this for less than 10 years now and we're already up to over 4,000 different mailings -- so you can see how complex things can get and how things can get lost between the cracks if you're not very, very careful. **This kind of organization helps set your agenda because you're setting deadlines, keeping the whole thing in constant motion, and putting yourself under some pressure to get it done.** That's incredibly important -- in fact, the more money you want to make, the more of this you have to do. That's true with all seven of these steps, of course. If you want to make millions and millions of dollars, then you need to put in a hell of a lot more work than if you just want to make hundreds of thousands of dollars.

A Quick Review

Let's do a quick recap of these seven steps. Step One is to create an affinity for and with the market. You really want to be friends with your customers and, in order to be friends with them, you have to understand them. People will continue to do business with companies that they believe really understand them.

Step Two is to send for other marketers' information, so you can see how they do things and find out what's out there. All the ideas you're looking for right now are being used by other people. It's a real shortcut to do this; not only do you get the

---

CHAPTER TWO

53

education you need, but when it comes time to develop your own material, you've got some great models to work from.

Step Three: Know what your customers want. Mostly what people want is new things that are easy; they want systems where everything is put together for them, all in one place. The better it sounds, the easier it sounds, the better it's going to sell. That's a truism in any market.

Step Four is to start small. This is great advice, but most entrepreneurs will never follow it. My wife and I only followed it because we were dead broke. That's it. If Eileen and I had had more money to spend back then, we would have screwed it all up and I wouldn't be here right now trying to share this with you. All we had was a few hundred bucks so we were forced to be frugal. All our decisions had to be limited by the money. We were forced to start by running small ads because that's all we could afford. **But to this day I'm so grateful for that because I see lots of people who go out and blow thousands of bucks when they would be better off if they'd started small and built their foundation with methods I've have talked about in this book.** You can think bigger as your confidence, knowledge, and experience increases.

Step Five is segmenting your customers. You need to get to know who your best customers are and you have to take better care of them than you do your other customers. You have to stay in touch with them on a regular basis. Try to develop a real bond or connection with your customers, so it's like any friendship. If you want to maintain a relationship and keep it growing, there has to be constant contact and you have to reach out and let your best customer know you're really trying to help them. That helps them feel better about you and, the better they feel about you, the more money they're willing to spend with you.

Step Six is: develop alliances with other smart marketers.

Nobody ever gets rich by themselves. When you study the lives of successful entrepreneurs, you'll always find that they had a whole lot of help from a whole lot of people along the way -- and nothing could be more true about my own success. Don't make the mistake that I see so many other people making. **Don't hide yourself away; go out there and try to find people that you can do a lot of business with, people who will also become your best friends.** There are so many people out there who have more knowledge than you do, people who have been through experiences that you're probably going to go through, so they're going to know what the pitfalls are. They're going to give you information and advice, suggestions and counsel to help you avoid some of things they've already gone through. In other words, they've already made their mistakes -- why should you make them again?

I thank God that I'm surrounded with people who are smarter than I am because they're constantly keeping me from making terrible mistakes. They've kept me from blowing this whole thing up many, many times. Like a lot of people who want to make a lot of money, I'm extremely ambitious and I tend to be very reckless at times and don't follow my own advice. Your friends will keep you from screwing up and they'll also keep you moving in the right direction.

Step Seven is, again, planning and organizing. You need this, so you can keep track of everything and be more successful. It's boring, but it's absolutely necessary if you want to make the most possible amount of money and the least number of mistakes. **It can also force you to keep the work flowing, especially if, say, you have to produce a product that you've already offered to your customers at a specific prepublication rate -- and they've already paid for that product.** Most of us are all jazzed and excited when we're writing that sales letter and making that initial offer, but we're less excited when it comes to actually creating the product. Well, this ensures that you get it done because you never, never want to fail to produce what someone has already paid good money for. Don't be afraid to make promises; just be sure to keep them.

In other words, you're creating the outline of the product within the sales letter that you're writing to sell the product. And if it's a brand new idea and something that really excites you, then that energy will be transferred over into the sales material, which is where you need it to be. When people are reading your sales material, you want them to be excited. **The best sales letters, the ones that have made us the most money over the years, were all written before there ever was a product or service to ship**. Take, for example, a product my friend Mike Lamb was working on as I was writing this book. First, he created what essentially was going to be the window dressing and the sales letter of the product, next, he'll go back and create the product based on what he's told his prospects in that sales letter.

There are so many people out there who are looking to find out how to create information products or to make money online. **There are many different people with many different approaches and perceptions that they're trying to share with other people and some people are getting lot of money for it.** In my case, I've decided to take this whole concept -- the knowledge that I've already acquired and the things that I've discovered on my own that work and don't work, and put them together in what's essentially a training book with the minute details of how to actually go out and start creating income online.

I'm not talking about somebody going out and making millions of dollars -- I'm just talking about somebody learning the essence of what you have to do in order to get somebody else to give you a check for the little effort that you put into it. Because if you start making money on something you're doing, you're more apt to start learning more about what you're doing so that you can make more money.

Here's the secret to turning that into a great business opportunity. This may sound sarcastic, but it's the absolute truth as I know it. **In addition to knowing what people want in the market -- that's Step Three up there -- you have to know what they don't want.** This will probably sound terrible, and I don't mean to be offensive, but in this market, people don't want to learn anything. There are exceptions, but the fact is that some of the products that really flopped for us over the years -- the ones that didn't make us a dime -- were our training products.

Now, here's how to make that into a great business opportunity. Remember, a great business opportunity is three things, that's all. You've got to have a product to sell, you've got to have sales material to sell it with, and you need a start-up manual that gives people the chance to order the sales material and tells them how to use it. What we do is go ahead and print all the sales material up for the distributor. We make it easy for them to become our distributor. **As a distributor, some of them will now actually pay attention to your product because you've appointed them as the joint owner.** They naturally want to know more. Eventually it will catch up to them; once you start putting some money in somebody's pocket, they change. They start paying attention to what you're doing and learning more about how to put more money in their pocket. I've seen money change people many, many times and, mostly, for the better.

Now, I don't mean that you change as in you turn into a Dr. Jekyll or Mr. Hyde all of a sudden. We're talking about the evolutionary change that takes place, as far as the learning curve goes. A lot of people in the opportunity market just don't want to learn anything, at least at first. What they want is the appearance of how to, without the how to. It's a hard concept to explain. Think of it this way: people are already frustrated in this marketplace. **As**

part of that frustration, they're totally overwhelmed -- so they just want you to put a complete system together for them. That's the part of the way you solve their biggest problem, which is the fact that's they're in emotional pain, they're frustrated, they're angry, they're confused. **So you come along and offer them a turnkey system that gives them a great product to sell, sales material to sell it with, and then you show them how to use that sales material.** Go out there, give them a website, show them what to do and, as long as you keep it simple and it's an exciting product with the potential to sell and make them a lot of money, they're on board with you 100%.

Now they're all jazzed and pumped up. They're interested in finding out more information and new ideas and new strategies; they want to discover what's out there. Now they're open and receptive to other deals you might want to offer them. **Some of the smartest marketers I know have pointed out that if you really do have a way to help people and you're not offering it to them, then you're doing them a disservice.** Once you create a list of customers -- people who have done business with you and trust you and like you -- your goal is obvious: you want to help them by doing more business with them. The questions of what to sell becomes easier and easier. You just keep looking for more things that are similar to what they bought from you the first time and then try to expand on that. It becomes so much easier as you go along.

Chapter Three

A-Z Success Formula: The First Few Steps

Next up, I'd like to share with you what I call my Rags-to-Riches, A-Z Success Formula. This is a list of 26 of the most important things that we've learned over the years, things that have made us the most amount of money. **I honestly believe that just one or two items on this list, if internalized and correctly applied in a passionate way, could actually grow your business by leaps and bounds.** So think of this as a smorgasbord, one of those giant fresh-food buffets. Although it's covered with all different kinds of foods, you just take what you like and leave the rest, making the plate of food that you want. I think that's the best way to approach this formula.

Secret A

Our first secret is becoming familiar with the market, something I've talked a lot about before. **Little did I know it at the time, but the reason Eileen and I were able to go from $300 to over $10 million in just four years was that we were already very familiar with the market.** Of course, we had the right help and there was an element of luck mixed in there, but it was the familiarity with the marketplace that helped us make all the money that we made and it's still helping us. We were customers for so many years that when it came time to produce our own opportunity, we already had an innate feel for the marketplace -- even though we weren't consciously able to communicate that clearly at the time. I can see this now only through hindsight. **There's no substitute for developing an intimate knowledge of the people that you want to serve, knowing them like they don't even know themselves.** Their hopes, their dreams, their desires, their fears, what makes them tick, what really keeps them up at night. The more you can know that marketplace, the better off you'll be.

I remember the very first product I ever bought; I even remember where I was, which is a grocery store that no longer exists. I was in the checkout aisle, bored to death, and there was a bunch of tabloids on a rack right next to me. I picked one up, thumbed through it, and I saw an ad by one of our competitors who's no longer in business. The headline was "$25,000 for a Few Hours' Work Doesn't Seem Fair." Once I got home, I tore the ad out, sent in my ten dollars, and waited by the mailbox.

I re-read the ad maybe 40 times while I was waiting for the product to come. **Just like most good opportunity ads, it was blind as a bat. It told you all the things that it wasn't, but it didn't ever tell you what it really was, so you had to send in your money to get the rest of the story.** That's one of the secrets in the opportunity market, people like to be teased that way. They like that anticipation, so blind ads really work great.

Coincidentally enough, the product turned out to be a book that showed you how to sell moneymaking books to the opportunity market. It was sold by someone out of Virginia who called himself John Christwall (I'm not sure that was really his name). It was a full-page ad, showing a woman standing on the left hand side. At the bottom were the order form and the ad itself. **It was a simple idea; it was a book much like the book I'm writing now, though without all the depth of knowledge that I'm including here, frankly.** But it was a formula, just like my A-Z formula I'm describing here.

Secret B

The second secret of my A-Z formula is something that not everybody has, but it's important: previous business experience. **Years ago, one of the things that used to keep me up at night was the fact that some of our distributers were making tens of thousands of dollars a month with our Dialing for Dollars book, while others weren't making a cent.** I've already told you about the man in Provo, Utah, who made $5 million a year before he cut our company out and started going on his own. But on the other hand, we had other people who were swearing that we had ripped them off, that we were selling them stuff that was no good. They'd tried it and it didn't work -- so it couldn't be any good, right?

Well, we knew it worked. Not only had it worked for us, we had people who were literally jumping in their car and driving over from several states away just to shake our hands and thank us for this book! And then, we had all kinds of wholesale orders coming in from around the country from people who were making money selling our products -- so we knew it was working.

The only common denominator we found was that the successful distributors had previous business experience. **That led me to develop a theory: while those people who were successful were still running into problems, obstacles, and challenges faced by all the people who claimed we were ripping them off, because they had previous business experience, <u>they were able to continue to test new things and they didn't just quit so easily</u>.** They weren't expecting some panacea; they hung with it enough to where they finally started making some serious money.

I don't think there's any substitute for business experience. **A seasoned businessperson is more apt to stay**

with something and not expect everything to be perfect. They know the value of what they bring to the table; they know the value of their time. Like the old joke goes, "the best part about being in business for yourself is the fact that you're your own boss…and the worst part about being in business for yourself is the fact that you're your own boss." People with previous business experience know how to flick their own switch. They know how to get themselves out of bed in the morning. They know how to keep themselves motivated so they're not just slacking off all day long and playing around. They don't have to have somebody standing over their shoulder all the time, telling them what to do next.

Secret C

That leads us to Secret C: get yourself a partner, especially if you don't have previous experience. **In our case, the synergy between Eileen and I made a huge difference.** I've already mentioned that I truly believe I would have blown the company up a number of times if it hadn't been for my wife because I was too immature, reckless, and wild -- and I had too much learning to do. Eileen is the Queen of Common Sense. She's very well grounded, very conservative. She didn't let me do a lot of the wild and crazy things I wanted to do during the 14 years she ran the company. She constantly held me back -- and that was the source of lots of fight between us. But somewhere along the line I did grow up a little bit and I adopted some of her conservative mentality.

Sometimes we need people who are smarter than we are, who have strengths in the areas that we're weak in, to help balance us and keep us focused on the right path. For me, that was Eileen and some of our key joint venture partners like Russ Von Hoelscher and Alan R. Bechtold and Dan Kennedy. Plain and simply, we need people. **I see too many entrepreneurs who are**

trying to do it all on their own and that's insane. They should be leaning hard on people who can help them. Certainly, we would have never made millions of dollars had we not done that.

Secret D

Secret D in my A-Z success formula is timing. We all know that the right idea at the right time is vitally important. **You've got to strike while the iron is hot and you've got to be able to identify things that are culturally, socially, or emotionally important to your audience.** And the neat thing is, there's always something new if you're looking for it, if you keep your mind focused. That's one of the things that people in the opportunity market desperately want -- whatever is new, whatever sounds interesting or hot. They love revolutionary, new technology. We were involved with computer bulletin boards in 1993, back when the electronic marketing thing was just getting off the ground, and that was hot for a while. When the Internet came along, we had a 12-year period where everything revolved around the Internet.

People are always looking for something that's hot and there always is something hot out there. I think their mentality is that they're always looking for something that's going to be the next big thing. They don't want to be left out, so they're always jumping on the newest bandwagon, thinking that it's going to be the next big thing. There are new things popping up all the time. Recently we've gotten involved with eBay. It was hot; it was on all the magazines, in all the magazines, it was on all the news programs. **Everywhere you looked, it was EBay! EBay! EBay! So we started developing programs to help people make money on eBay.** It's hot, it's current. You've got to look for things that people are talking about, things that are in the news. You've got to develop your programs, your products, and services around things that sound new, different, revolutionary, cutting-edge.

CHAPTER THREE

At the very least, your customers and prospects need to have the perception that it's new. **There's plenty of old stuff out there that you can give a new twist to and offer up to your client.** Right now we've got a program out there based on what we call "chain reaction marketing." But the truth is, it's really something called viral marketing that's been around for about a decade now on the Internet. All we did was put a new, more positive name on it. It'll be new to the people who hear it the first time, so you're not ripping off or misleading them. I think that's the thing that most marketers miss. In the Internet marketing world we're marketing to all these people online, trying to create revenue. We've got our ugly websites selling moneymaking CD series; we're doing all these things specifically to show people how to create money on the Internet. Now that's just one marketing vehicle -- but the amazing thing is that there are so many people who are just now venturing onto the Internet. **They have no idea of the availability, of the technology, of the power, or the resources that are here. So when you bring something new to that marketplace, you're actually the benchmark, the launch point for that particular person about this information -- even if it's a repackaging of an old idea!**

The same holds true with everything in the opportunity market. There are people that have never been in the opportunity market, they don't know that it even exists until they hear what we're talking about -- and it opens up a whole new way of thinking for them. Remember that! **Just because you're sick and tired of a promotion that you've been running for a while, that doesn't mean it's not new to some of the people you're exposing it to.** This is one of the big mistakes that marketers make. They'll have a promotion that's still generating nice profits, but it's been out there for a while, it's old hat, they don't like to talk about it anymore. They're sick and tired of it themselves and so they pull it far earlier than they should. They could just leave it running and let it continue to produce profits for them on a consistent basis -- but they scrap it way too fast. They forget that just because they're sick of it, that doesn't mean everybody else is sick of it. There will always be those who are brand new, who are becoming exposed to it for the first time ever. To them it's exciting, fresh, captivating -- and that's the only thing that matters.

Secret E

Next, you need to find the right help. In our case, we found a marketing wizard to help us get on the right track. After our first six months, we got a letter in the mail from marketing consultant Russ Von Hoelscher. Russ simply included a brochure on his consulting services and said. "Look, I like what you guys are doing. I've seen your materials and I think I can help you." Then I called the number he provided and Russ started working with us. **At that time he had over 20 years of experience in the opportunity market, so his experience became our experience.** We were just like little Forrest Gumps: whatever Russ said, we did -- and lo and behold, within our first nine months of working with him, we went from $16,000 a month to almost a $100,000 a week. He'd already gone where we wanted to go, he'd figured out all of the problems that we had yet to figure out. By simply leaning hard on him, we were able to make a lot more money in a faster period of time than we would have any other way.

Soon after we heard from Russ, he started flying to Kansas and spending the weekends working with us. We would pick him up on a Friday night at the Wichita airport, he'd stay over as a guest in our home, and then we'd take him back to the airport on Sunday morning to fly home. On the way to Goessel that first time, he told me -- I'll never forget where I was when he said it, because it just really changed my thinking -- **"In this business, all it takes is one good idea to make a million bucks."** That was the first time I'd ever heard that, but I was ready for that message

---

and it stuck in my mind.

Very soon after that, we had one idea, just one idea, that made us well over a million dollars. It was a simple idea and yet it resonated with our customers. **They embraced it, they bought it like crazy, they loved it, and it made us a lot of money.** Here's how it went. Russ was charging us $2,500 every weekend that he came down to work with us. Plus, we paid his airfare, all his other travel expenses, and he also charged us money for every hour we were on the telephone with him and for special copywriting that he did for us and special joint ventures that we did with him -- although we never really used that terminology back then. We immediately saw value in what he was doing and what he could bring to the table because we knew that it takes money to make money. Russ has helped us make a lot of money over the years, but he's also been well paid for his time.

Russ became like a 'Dutch uncle' with us, he saw us as a couple of young ambitious kids and he just took us under his wing. It's about more than money because he really tried to help us in every way. **He tried to help us not only from the business side of things with marketing and product development and getting us involved in direct mail, but he also helped us on the personal side because, at that time, we had struggled with poverty for so many years.**

We didn't know what it was like to be rich. Once the money really started pouring in, it was such a shock to our systems -- and Russ had already experienced that before. He'd made and lost millions of dollars himself earlier on. When the money first comes in, sometimes if you're not careful, you end up like those lottery winners that hit it big and don't know what to do with the money when it comes in. It creates some emotional and personal problems. **Russ helped us deal with all of the aspects of our success**. It's extremely important to have someone like him to help you early on.

Secret F

Often, when people hear our story, they ask, "What is it that Russ helped you do that caused you to make so much money in such a short period of time?" **And the answer to that question is direct mail -- Secret F in our A-Z marketing system.** Until we began working with him, we were just running space advertisements. Russ helped us get started with direct mail, he introduced us to our list manager (who's also our list broker) and, within a short period of time, we were mailing out millions of pieces of mail every year. That let us reach so many more people in a more powerful way than the space advertising we were using. It's because of direct mail that we've made our real fortune. It's an exciting medium. **Once you start getting into direct mail, you'll never go back to any other medium in a serious way.** You might still do other things when it comes to marketing and advertising, but direct mail is such an exciting way to make money. That may be hard to understand, but someday I hope you, the reader, can experience the thrill of sending out millions of pieces of direct mail and then getting tens of thousands of them back, with cash, checks, money orders, and credit card authorizations in them.

Most direct mail experts tell you to go to the reference section of your library and go through the Standard Rating Data Services (SRDS) volume to find a good list manager. The SRDS is the big trade reference book that contains all the mailing lists that are for rent; they do a write-up on each of the lists and the list managers and you can do your research there pretty simply. But I've got a simpler way that works better for me. **The problem is that all the big list managers make all their listings look the same. They're all trying to get you to rent those lists, so they say all kinds of great things. You don't know who to**

---

believe. So we've got a couple of good mailing list brokers who go out and find us lists to rent. We trust their opinions, they're working on our behalf.

We know that not all the lists we test are going to work well -- as a matter of fact, only a small percentage of the lists that we test actually do work. But since we're constantly testing new lists, we're finding that small percentage that work and then those lists are added to our arsenal. **Over time we've developed enough mailing lists that we're mailing fifty thousand pieces every week.** Some of those fifty thousand names are new, but a lot of them are on mailing lists that we've been using for years.

You work with a couple of brokers who have good reputations, who are honest people with integrity, and you let them go out there and stay on the telephone all day, smiling and dialing and talking to other list managers and other list brokers. That's really how simple it is with us. **They're looking out for us, trying to do everything possible to get us good mailing lists that we'll keep using and re-renting from them because they get a nice little percentage of it -- I think it's 15-17%.** We're more than happy to pay that because they're providing a good moneymaking service for us.

Although you're usually required to rent a minimum of 5,000 names from a list, that doesn't mean you have to mail to all 5,000 at once and we never do. We'll rent ten different lists, which represent 50,000 names, but we may only actually test a couple of thousand from each list. If it works, we'll go back and mail the other 3,000 and then we'll go back and get all of the remainder counts. They may have put up 20,000 names during that quarter, and we'll be forced to rent 5,000 as a test. **We'll test 2,000 as a mailing and if that works we'll quickly go back and mail the other 3,000, plus we'll get the other 15,000 they're offering.** The next time they come out with another quarterly list, we may still just take little baby steps until we're real comfortable with them.

Now, sometimes these list owners or managers will give you only the best names on the list. Those names will work like gangbusters for you, then you'll go back and rent the other 45,000 real quick -- and the other names won't even be from the same list you tested to begin with. So there are some sharks swimming in the oceans that you have to watch out for. If you work with a good mailing list broker, they'll keep you away from the dishonest people as much as they can.

Since we first got into direct mail, in 1989, we've tested every kind of format and price points. Different things have worked for us at different times. When Eileen ran the company, she had a rule: we always had to break even on the front end. So whatever money we brought in on new customer acquisition had to recover the cost of the mailing.

Now, little did she know that I was sort of doctoring up the books -- I was working with the numbers guy and the data that she was seeing wasn't always accurate. Why? Because I knew the companies that make the most money in direct response marketing are companies that always go negative on the front end. What do I mean by that? **It's simple, it just means that you don't always make a profit or even break even on the very first sale you make to a customer.** I never looked at it as losing money, I looked at it as an investment towards future profits, the cost of doing business.

That's the way the companies that are making the most money in this marketplace are doing it. **They're all investing huge amounts of money toward future profits and I knew that.** I also knew that Eileen was playing it way too conservative and so, when Eileen stepped down and I stepped up, I started doing some of the very aggressive things that a lot of the biggest direct response marketers are doing. For instance, on one $50 promotion I was

---

more than happy to pay $500 to acquire the right customer, so we were going negative. **I learned a lot of lessons by doing that. For example, that you can be too aggressive, you can spread it out too fast.** I ended up having some serious cash flow problems -- but that was a whole other story.

As it happens, I think most people aren't aggressive enough. Most people should be willing to invest more money in front-end, new customer acquisition, and not worry about breaking even or showing a profit. **All of the money's on the back end, so what you have to do is get as many customers as possible to raise their hands the first time and buy something from you or at least send away for something you offered.** Build your list as big as you can because the real business starts after that first sale. That's when you start kicking in all of your back-end marketing and that's where all your profits come from.

The front end is a tough business. That's the case anytime you're trying to do business with people who have no existing relationship with you. They don't know you and they don't trust you, so it's always going to be difficult to make sales to those people at a profit. **This is a very important lesson to learn because you could be focused on just trying to break even and lose the opportunities for all the future business because you've got a program that ultimately is going to make you a lot of money.** If you're going to be aggressive with your marketing, then for every sale that you make at a $100 level, you'd better be willing to spend two or three hundred dollars to make that initial sale. Now you've got a deficit for every customer you're bringing in, so you've got to make up that other money as fast as you possibly can so that you break even as quickly as possible. That becomes the game. **Once you break even, then you've got that customer for free; that's how I look at it.** You've got somebody who trusts you and you know what they're interested in because they're voting with their checkbook. When somebody sends you $100 or $1,000, what they're really saying is, "Hey! I want what you have so bad I'm willing to give you my hard-earned money."

When you get to break-even, you've got the customer for free, so you want to get there as fast as you can -- but you may not be able to do it on the initial sale. It may take two or three sales, which you'll have to make as quickly as you can. That becomes the game, so that you can break even and get that customer free. **Now, one thing that you have to do with direct mail is to track the lifetime value of each customer.** We have many offers that go out on a consistent basis to all of our best customers, so we're constantly trying to do more and more business with those people. We have a continual front end marketing campaign that brings us new customers and then we have an ongoing campaign that re-sells to them again and again. Some of the people we sell to have been on our list for Lord knows how long -- some have probably been there from the very beginning.

The average customer has bought from us maybe four or five times. At the beginning you're sitting there thinking, "Okay, I'm going to go out and I'm put this offer on the table. I know that if I can create a customer with this offer then, based on my previous success, that customer becomes worth ten, twenty, thirty times that amount."

Why does this work as well as it does? Well, with the opportunity market -- and I know I've said this before -- you're working with rabid buyers. You're dealing with people who will come back again and again and buy more of whatever you're selling. That's one thing that makes this marketplace so exciting. Therefore, whatever it takes to get that customer one time, to develop a relationship with them, to let them know who you are and to give them a taste of what it is that you sell -- that's just the first step in a lifelong series of re-purchases they'll make from you. And as you educate your customer, the offers can

---

become larger, more extensive, and, obviously, more valuable. In other words, you can keep asking for more and more money.

The main thing you need to do is make sure that the first product or service you sell to the customer is top quality, so it really makes an impression on them. From that point forward they're going to be more apt to buy from you again. **Many marketers out there base their business on this marketing or profit funnel concept, where you sell somebody something small and then you ramp them up.** Maybe you start with a $17 product, then proceed to a $47 product, then on to $97 and $147 products. Later on it may be $1,000, $2,000, or $5,000. Now, you can start a new customer with a big-ticket item without much fallout if you're very careful, but I'd recommend offering a mix of different prices so that people can start where they're comfortable. If I could do nothing but sell products and services for $3,000 or $5,000, of course I'd do it -- but that's not entirely reasonable. We do have products and services within our overall mix that sell for prices that high, but there are a lot of people in our customer base who just don't have that kind of money, so it's nice to have a range of different prices of products and services.

Be careful to keep offering a mix of products because, once you get a taste for selling things that are high dollar, you'll never want to go back. One of my weak areas used to be the fact that I was hesitant to try selling information for thousands of dollars. But once I broke through that fear, after 7 or 8 years in business, all I wanted to do was sell things at high prices. **This hurt the company because it really is better to have an overall mix that just about any customer can afford; so I learned that lesson quickly.** But don't hesitate to offer high-dollar products because you'll always have some percentage of customers who can afford them and who are willing to pay for them. If you don't offer high-dollar products to these people, you're losing money.

Chapter Four

A-Z Success Formula: Secrets G-K

For ease of discussion, I've broken my set of A-Z Marketing Success Formula secrets into fifths. In the previous chapter, I covered Secrets A-F; in this chapter I'll discuss the next five, which I call Secrets G-K.

Secret G

Secret G is this: you have to keep two different checkbooks for your business, at least in the beginning. At M.O.R.E., Inc. we did this only for the first few years, but it was imperative for us -- it helped us establish a certain discipline that we've maintained to this day. When we used this method, we made sure that whatever came in that day -- whether it was $50 or $50,000 -- we took thirty percent of that money and we put it into a separate account that was used only for advertising. **We disciplined ourselves every single day to make that sure no matter how many bills we had to pay, we always had enough money to cover our advertising.** Some people do that with taxes, too.

With us, there was awareness from Day One that if we didn't constantly make sure that our money was allocated towards advertising, we weren't going to grow the business. **To this day, our Number One priority is to keep our 50,000 front-end pieces going out on a weekly basis.** Every single week, we know we're going to be bringing in so many hundreds of new customers or so

---

many thousands of new leads. That's the first part of our marketing machine -- and then we also make sure that we're constantly re-mailing to our existing customers on an ongoing basis. We're raining mail on their heads. We're staying in touch with them. We're selling them more and more stuff. It's a real commitment to continue to funnel more and more money back into the things that made you the money in the first place, but it's also necessary.

A Slight (But Instructive) Diversion

The number of mailings the average customer on our list gets depends on which part they're on, since it's segmented. In some cases, our best customers might hear from us as often as several hundred times during the year. **We do a lot of two-step lead generation campaigns where we're constantly separating the smaller group of our best customers from the bigger herd**. We're still marketing to the bigger group, but the smaller group gets a series of ongoing, systematic repeat mailings. If they keep raising their hands, they're going to get a lot of mail. There may be as many as 14-20 different follow-ups for each of those campaigns. Add in all the voice mail blasting that we do and they could hear from us two or three other times a year.

How do we keep track of it all? Well, we've got people who we've been working with for a long time and we meet every week. We're all in-house except for our mailing house and printer -- and representatives from each are there at the meetings. **We also have staff members who really understand what we do because we've been doing it for so long.** All our mailings are numbered and it's all dated; it's a system that we just worked out and have grown into over a period of time. It didn't just happen overnight. **Here's what's behind the system: an awareness that we have to keep new offers going out on a regular basis.** In the past, we used to worry that we were going to be "slamming" our customers too often. That used to be something we argued constantly: are we hitting them too hard? Should we let up on them? We've gotten past all that and what we've found is that there seems to be no end to the number of times you can go after your best customers and make them offers. I think a lot of marketers are too afraid of that, like we were -- we were frozen in fear for a good decade, worried that we were going to mail to our customers too often. **But the more we mail, the more money we make.** Of course, you've got to have the people on your list trained not to think that every time you send them a piece of mail, you're trying to sell them something. Think of it as educating them about you. Everything you're sending is part of that education.

I think it's funny how many times I've had customers come up to me at seminars, complaining about all the mail that we send them, and I look at their buying patterns and their histories and I see that they just keep right on buying more and more stuff. I love what Dan Kennedy taught me early on: he said, "Look T.J, it doesn't matter who you piss off; it just matters who you sell. So don't worry about pissing off some of your customers." And I love what Brad Antin said, too: "If your refunds aren't high enough, then you're not selling hard enough." **Too many marketers love to brag about how low their refunds are. Well, that's nothing to be proud of -- it just means you're not selling aggressively enough.**

People who care about their customers, who want to keep them for life, are afraid to do this for fear of losing them. But there's no way you're going to keep a lot of them for life anyway -- people get obsessed with buying at one time or another and while they're obsessed you have to sell them as hard and as fast as you can. Do not worry so much about whether you're going bother them so much that they're going to leave you.

As I mentioned earlier, many of our promotions are two-step lead generation -- so we're constantly offering free

---

CHAPTER FOUR   75

reports, free audio CDs, free DVDs, free tele-seminars, and other items to get people to raise their hands. Many of our offers are designed to separate that small herd out of the larger herd so we can follow up and do a series of sequence campaigns to that small group, market to the bigger group aggressively, and just keep the whole thing in motion so the smaller groups are getting sequenced mailings.

Another big mistake a lot of marketers make is that they just give up on their prospects too soon. So somebody will raise their hand and they'll show an interest, they'll attend a free tele-seminar, they'll buy this and they'll buy that -- but if you don't send them enough follow-up materials, if you're not constantly on them, you may lose them. You have to keep asking them over and over again to buy from you.

I think this makes a lot of sense because, if somebody is interested in who you are and what you have, then they're going to be more interested in learning more about you and how you can put more money in their pocket or to help them have a better life. What Brad Antin said is so apropos to successful businesspeople. **Everybody has people decide "This is not what I want!" and you have to give them their money back -- but you shouldn't complain.** It's a no-hassle, 100%-guarantee world that we live in and you don't want to deal with somebody who doesn't want your stuff. So you can give their money back, get them off your list, and know they're never going to hassle you again.

Realize, though, that in the opportunity market, people are so skeptical that they may test you -- sometimes without even being aware of it. So if someone sends something back and you give them a refund, don't necessarily take them off your list right away; they may come back and buy something from you later, knowing that you have integrity. Here's what I mean: about ten years ago we had a seminar that we were selling for about $5,000, and at one point I asked the audience a question, trying to teach them the value of long-term relationships: "How many of you in this room have ever bought something from M.O.R.E., Inc. and wanted your money back?" About a third of the hands went up. **You see, they're constantly testing you; they're constantly trying to decide whether they can believe you and, sometimes, the only way they can tell is by your actions.** When you give them their money back when they're not happy, you're solidifying your relationship with them.

In the same situation, a lot of marketers say to themselves, "That customer doesn't want us; they'll never want us again." I myself was very immature when we first got started. I had so much learning to do and I took it personally when somebody wanted their money back. It was like an insult to me. I loved my product like every salesman should. I loved what we were doing. I knew it was a good program and, when somebody wanted their money back, it was like a slam on me -- so I had an immature attitude and I used to get ticked off when people asked for a refund. The same thing is true for a lot of us who are on the Internet and have someone jump off our lists. **I don't think you should give up on people that soon, especially in the opportunity market where you're dealing with the heavy emotional issues that cause people to buy from you to begin with.** You have to realize, there's a general sense of unhappiness that flows through this marketplace; if people were truly happy, truly satisfied with their lives, they wouldn't have such an insatiable desire to get rich in the first place.

There's a great book by Nobel Prize winner Eric Hoffer called The True Believer. **In the first sentence of the first chapter, it says that it all starts with a frustrated person -- and there could be nothing truer when it comes to the opportunity market.** These are people who are frustrated to begin with; they're not happy. They all want to get rich quick; they all want to make a lot of money overnight; they have delusions of grandeur. They believe in secrets; they believe that there's an easy way and it's all going to come raining out of the sky. If that sounds negative, I'm sorry; it's not a judgment, it's an observation. **That kind of emotion causes people to Federal Express their orders and, in some cases, to wire them through Western Union because they're in such a hurry to get whatever you have.** That same emotion also causes them, sometimes, to pick up the phone and call you every name in the book, to abuse you and your staff verbally, to demand their money back, and threaten to take you to the Attorney General's office and the FTC. It's all part of life.

Secret H

This is one of the most important elements of success: back-end marketing. To me, this is the real business. I see too many people putting all their emphasis on front-end marketing, which is illogical. First of all, it's really hard to make any kind of profit on the front end. We've done it -- we're doing it right now -- but it's not the norm. **Normally, the real money comes from doing more business with the customers that you already have; that's going to make you rich.** So we put all the focus on back-end marketing, unlike many of our competitors

So let's simplify the back end, especially for people just starting to understand what this whole marketing realm is all about. A "back end" is something additional that you sell to a customer you've already converted. Actually, it's a whole bunch of somethings additional because the goal is to attract the best people as new customers and then continue to sell to them again and again. **Every time you resell to an established customer, the profits can be higher and higher.** The expense lies in getting that new customer initially, so the goal is to bring in as many new customers as you can and resell them all the products and services you can.

It sounds like a daunting task, but it's fun -- and that's the thing that people don't realize. When you have an existing group of customers who already know you -- who trust you, whom you understand intimately -- then trying to decide what products and services to sell to them becomes much easier. **Because you're focused on them and now, instead of being confused about what to sell, your only real challenge is this: what are the few things I can sell that will produce the largest amount of profit?** Your decision-making becomes easier and it's easier to develop products and services for people you really care about. And you should care about them because they're the people who are paying your bills. They're continuing to give you money, financing your dreams, and helping pay for your financial goals. So you're really reaching out as one friend reaches out to another and you're trying to give it all you've got.

Once you create a customer, it's easier to go back and sell to them because you and they have a relationship. **You can take the same promotions you have going out to new customers and, without changing a thing, you'll get double the response, at least, from your best customers.** Sometimes you'll get as much as 10-20 times the response, because when people trust you, they're more open and receptive to giving you money. The biggest challenge of new customer acquisition is the fact that they don't trust you, so they're less apt to do business with you. The good news is that once you do have customers who have already done business with you once, they're likely to do business with you again.

That's where the passion lies in doing business, for me, because that's where the real business is. **The front end is a necessary evil; I call it an "evil" because it's difficult to make money with it. Oftentimes you're not making money at all -- you're actually going negative on the front end.** You can spend a lot of money on the front end, hoping to get a customer, and it simply may not develop the way you want it to. I became a reverse

---

millionaire a while back because I got too aggressive -- and that was a lesson I had to learn just once. I wasn't watching my numbers carefully enough; I was actually spending far too much money on every new customer I was bringing in and it got to the point where I couldn't pay my suppliers, I was having trouble meeting payroll, and I was having to go talk to bankruptcy attorneys just to explore my options. I was drinking milk and eating crackers because that's all I could handle. But most people are pushing at the other end. **For every crazy and wild entrepreneur like I was back then, there are probably hundreds or thousands of other people who could be doing more.** They should be marketing more aggressively both on the front end, to acquire new customers, and on the back end, to resell to their old customers.

There's no real formula regarding how much you should apply to the front end vs. the back end to maximize the amount of money you're trying to extract from a customer. I think it depends on the individual marketplace and your actual promotion. You can be as aggressive as you want to be, as long as you're just testing small groups of prospects. I think the real answer to that question is. Do you have a back-end product or service that's directly tied to what they brought from you on the front end? **If the answer is yes, then if you can tie your back-end promotion with your front-end so that it's a natural, logical up-sale that's directly related to what you sold them the first time, then you should be fine.** If there's enough money and profit in that back-end sale, then what you want to do is test small, so if you lose everything on that test you're not losing it all.

That's the smart way to approach it. **Always develop back-end offers; always have a good idea of what you're going to sell them next after they buy that initial product or service from you.** The closer that you can marry the two together, the better. One of the ways we do that is with two-tier distributorships, where we bring people in as distributors for a product or service. Now they're all excited and, suddenly we have a master distributorship opportunity. It lets them come in at a higher level, where they're able to get more money on every transaction. It's closely related to what they bought the first time, so it's a natural logical step for them to take. It makes sense and, therefore our conversion levels are higher. We're able to convert as many as 50% of all of those initial buyers who come in at a lower price point.

Generally, with brand new customers, you can't ask for a lot. They don't have any trust developed with you. It would be foolish to try to sell them something big and expensive, in most cases -- and of course we've done it. We've tested it and, in some applications it works; but in general, it's foolish to ask a brand new customer to spend thousands of dollars with you. **The smart thing is to take them through a series of very logical, closely-related steps that lead to that additional money.** Once they've bought something from you and you've treated then right, they trust you. They're more willing and able to go ahead and make the commitment, to give you the larger sum of money.

I'd like to re-emphasize the need to make sure that you're always testing small groups with your back-end marketing, so you're not really spending a huge amount of money on a product or service that might end up failing if sold to your initial front-end customers. Now, a lot of us hate to test, but like front-end marketing, it's a necessary evil. Of course, the more successful somebody is, the more they tend to feel that they don't have to test things -- and I've fallen for that myself, when I actually knew better. I've lost tens of thousands of dollars by not practicing what I'm preaching right here because I just said, "Oh, hell! We don't have to test; it'll work!" Sometimes you have a gut reaction to something based on past experiences, or based on ego, or based on somebody else's input -- but that doesn't necessarily have anything to do with that product's relationship to the customer

---

because you don't know what the customer is going to do, or how they'll react. Sometimes your gut feeling is wrong, so you test.

Here's what you do. You start out testing every new idea you have, to your very best customers first. First of all, by doing that you'll never lose money -- your best customers will buy anything from you, as long as they know that if they're not happy, they'll get their money back. You could sell them a box of rocks, if they knew they could get their money back if they wanted. **So you test your idea to your best customers first and then slowly start rolling it out to the rest of your customer list; and then, if it's still profitable, you use it for new customer acquisition.** You turn it into a lead generating campaign, a two-step new-customer-acquisition front-end marketing plan. There's a Zig Ziglar quote my wife and I like, it's really our mantra, and we actually put it on the back cover of the first product we ever developed. Since then it's sort of become an overall theme for our company: **"You can have anything in life you want, if you'll simply help enough other people get what they want."**

Secret I

This one involves forming a habit of constant front-end promotion. Your pool of customers is always going to shrink through attrition; people will die, lose interest, or move away, so you have to replenish the pond constantly. **You have to have at least one front-end promotion going all the time and, ideally more; though more than a few is hard to hard to manage.** Back when I was teetering on the edge of bankruptcy, I was trying to manage two front end promotions at the same time; that was part of my downfall.

What works best is to have one front-end promotion that consistently brings in a steady flow of brand new first time

---

customers and then have a series of back-end promotions that are out there bringing in more business from existing customers. <u>A lot of people fail on this very important principle</u>. They don't have a consistent way to bring in brand new customers or they do it haphazardly, sporadically. Business gets a little bad and all of a sudden they start running a bunch of promotions to bring in new customers. Then they stop and work those customers for a while, until business gets bad again. Then they go back out there and repeat that same crazy insane marketing.

What's better is that every single week, every single month, you run your promotion, space ad, or whatever it may be. It should be your most profitable promotion and you should constantly be testing new things. Your front end's always evolving. With us, we make sure we always send out those 50,000 pieces of direct mail -- week in, week out.

Even in the retail market, people are too focused on the front end. **They run all that advertising to get new customers and then forget about selling to existing customers again.** This is one of the reasons it's so exciting to be in the opportunity market -- because it's filled with competitors who don't understand the value of selling to people on the back end. They're trying to make all their money on those first sales and they're just not treating their customers well. They're not building relationships with them and they're not developing specific back-end related products and services to sell to those people. That's insane, but it's also one of the great things for those few people that want to step up to bat and do it right. **There are millions and millions of dollars on the table, just waiting to be made and I'm living proof that it can be done.**

Secret J

Secret J is essentially making sure that you have great

resources and the right suppliers. I see too many people who are what I call pennywise and dollar foolish. They're looking for the cheapest prices for everything and they're constantly shopping around and tapping a variety of different suppliers for all of their needs. Say, for instance, they'll have 4-5 different printers and, every time they need some printing done, they'll try to get bids from all of them. They may do the same with audio and video duplication companies or any of their other suppliers. They're not loyal to any of them; they're just price shopping. **Well, one of the secrets of our success is that the suppliers we work with are more like employees or staff members.** We continue to do business with the same suppliers over and over again. We don't always get the best price, but while price is important to us -- we're not trying to be foolish or make stupid decisions here -- what we're looking for are suppliers that will give us all three of the things we want. **We need great price, great service, and great turnaround time, too.** We bring these people into our office once a week; they're in our management meetings because they're an integral part of our business. We try to look out for them because we look at them as an extension of our companies -- and they go out of their way to help us.

They're trying to keep their costs down because they know that's important to us, but they're also trying to give us the best services and the best quality and helping us think things through. Our mailing house comes to our meetings every week; our representative's bringing us different mailings she sees and different technologies we're not aware of. They're constantly looking for ways of increasing the value of the services they provide to us. My printer is the same way and my duplication company is always looking for ways to give us more value.

One of the greatest relationships you can have is with people who have knowledge of other resources, people who are successful in business, who are using other vendors, and are willing to share those relationships with you. The more you befriend these people, the more they're going to do things to look out for you. Now, suppliers are just one aspect of that. **You can also develop joint venture relationships with other people who have the knowledge, experience, and skills that you lack.** They've gone where you want to go, they've made their mistakes, and now they can help you to avoid those mistakes. We've surrounded ourselves with people who are smarter than we are, who are more talented than we are, and they fill all the gaps we have within our own company. I'll talk more about joint ventures in a later section.

Secret K

Become a marketing junkie. There's a book that's sold millions of copies because it's got a jazzy title that people like: it's called "Do What You Love, and the Money Will Follow." I think it sells well because it appeals to a certain laziness people have, despite the fact that the title doesn't make much sense. After all, what people really love is to screw off; they love to just take it easy, to relax, eat at nice restaurants, and sleep in nice hotels. **I think it's better to find out what brings you the largest amount of money and then to fall in love with that.** By and large, what brings us the largest amount of money is marketing. All the things you do to acquire new customers and re-sell to them as long as you can, as often as you can, for as much profit as you can -- that's the thing to fall in love with. Like chess, marketing takes a day to learn and a lifetime to master.

The biggest element I try to focus on is relationship building because, if you can build a relationship with somebody, they're easier to manipulate (and I use that term in a positive way). **It's a lot easier to get those people to do what it is you want them to do. As long as it really helps them, then they need to be manipulated.** Hell, I've needed to be manipulated. A friend once

---

said to me, "T.J., if somebody would have told me 25 years ago what I was going to have to go through to get to where I am today, I would have hung myself." And I understand because I feel the same way. People lied to me in the beginning or they misled me or they told me what I wanted to hear. I wanted to become a multimillionaire-- and thank God there were people who came along telling me I could do it, that it wasn't going to be that difficult, it was going to be a piece of cake, no problem, go for it, go for it. Later, I found out that there's a tremendous price to pay and, the more money you want to make, the larger the price you've got to pay.

When I see a word like "manipulate," I view it in a lot of positive ways. I think that all selling is somewhat manipulative to begin with, but I also think some of us can't handle the truth and we need people to mislead us just a little bit so that we can stay on the right path. I don't mean to be sarcastic about this -- and I don't mean to sound like a weirdo about it, either -- **but some of the greatest things have happened to me because somebody manipulated me and I got in over my head before I knew all the problems and challenges I would ultimately have to overcome**. I was led to believe that it was a lot simpler than it really was, so that I could move forward on the path.

But back to becoming a marketing junkie. The very first thing you have to do is make a very strong commitment. First comes the hunger, the desire to set the goal that you're going to learn everything you can about marketing. It's worth it; this is one thing that can make you rich and it's your meal ticket for life. **It can make you all the money that you ever want, need, and deserve -- if you'll just learn the right skills.**

Once somebody is deeply committed, once they decide that come hell or high water they're going to learn everything they can about marketing, they're going to be willing to invest in various programs and seminars. **There are so many marketing experts out there sharing their greatest tips, tricks, and strategies for making more money.** It's something that we want to share and there are so many wonderful programs on the market right now. Check into them, send off for marketing materials, and set up swipe files. See how other people are selling their products and services; one thing always leads to another once you set that goal to become a marketing junkie.

What are some of the telltale signs you've become a marketing junkie? If you're spending thousands and thousands of dollars on all kinds of books, programs, and tapes, you might be a marketing junkie. If your whole life becomes marketing and you can't get it out of your head, you might be a marketing junkie. If it's 3:00 AM and you're still thinking and dreaming up new ways to make more money -- well, you might be a marketing junkie.

Chapter Five

A-Z Success Formula: Secrets L-P

We're now ready for Secret L, which is learning how to write copy that sells. **There's no more important skill in our business than the ability to write a sales letter that will get people so excited that they'll send you their money.** There's no greater feeling when you can do it right, either. It's a feeling of being in control of your destiny since, after all, as entrepreneurs we're stepping out there with the courage that we're going to do this without the security and safety blanket of a regular job and a paycheck. It took me a long time to learn to do this well and I think the same is true for most entrepreneurs.

Even during those ten years when I was cutting my teeth, while I was learning everything that I had to learn, I realized something very important: **that when you're writing copy to people who already trust you and have a good relationship with you, you don't have to be the best copywriter in the world to make nice profits selling to them.**

For years I was forced to use expensive outside copywriters to do all of our front-end material. It bothered me that I wasn't a good enough copywriter to do my own new customer acquisition, but I wasn't -- and if you're like I was, remember that there are plenty of copywriters who can help you with that end. **But I would encourage you to remember this: once you gather a group of customers who have bought from you once, start writing to them yourself.** Craft offers they like, keep working on different sales letters, and, not only will your copywriting skills improve, the more money you'll make.

Now, keep this in mind: while I do believe you should hire outside copywriters if you really need help, I think too many people become dependent on those copywriters. **I don't care how skilled these top guns are: <u>they're never going to put as much effort and energy into it as you are</u>.** It does take a while to learn how to master this skill, but you can always make more money writing your own copy than you would by hiring copywriters to do it all for you. I think not learning this skill is a big mistake that a lot of people make. It's such a great tool in your marketing arsenal.

In the beginning you have to emulate other people. **This was a tip that was given to me by the great Gary Halbert; he suggested that you take the best ad or sales letter you can find and re-write it in your own handwriting as many times as you can in order to get the feel and the language of copywriting down.** It's as though you're channeling the copywriter who wrote that particular copy. You're not thinking creatively, you're just going through the process of writing copy and you're basically training your brain to do that. Personally, I used Joe Carbo's Lazy Man's Way to Riches ad to train myself. I probably wrote that thing close to a hundred times over a period of 3-4 months -- to the point where I had it all memorized. This single one-page ad, 2,000-3,000 words long, made Joe Carbo millions of dollars. Rewriting it so many times really did help implant the language of good direct response, the flow of it, into my brain.

What made that sales letter perform for Joe Carbo? Well, first of all, Joe had a lot of experience already in the business before he wrote the first word of that ad. It had been an idea that had been percolating in his head for a while. In my experience, an idea sometimes does have to percolate for a long time but, as the story goes, he got to the point where all of a sudden he was ready to do it and he basically did just write it all from the top down. He actually woke up in the middle of the night, went to his kitchen table, and hand-wrote that ad. There's a certain power to writing sales letters when you're fired up. **There's an energy you get when you're firing on all cylinders, when an idea is fresh and new to you; that's why you should always write the sales letter first, before you develop the product because, by the time you get the product developed, there goes all your energy and now the last thing you want to do is write a sales letter about it.** But the sales letter obviously is the most important element of the whole process. If you build your product around the sales letter and you write the sales letter when the idea is fresh and new and exciting, it'll make you a lot more money.

While you're in the moment, inspired by your idea, don't go work on the product: go work on the sales letter and tell the person that you want to buy this product every single thing the product's going to do for them. **Tell them all the features and benefits, all the elements -- because then you've not only got an outline for the product, you've also got a level of excitement going.** That's what the Lazy Mans Way to Riches is all about. That ad makes you want to buy the product when you're done reading it. You get excited.

Now, Joe made all of his millions on the front end. The market has changed since then, so you can't do that today, but it worked like gangbusters for him. I just love that ad; <u>I would encourage anyone reading this book to go find that ad, read it, and study it</u>.

Secret M

The next secret in my Rags to Riches success formula involves developing skills in product development. It's something

---

that you should work on every single day. So many people come to me and say, "I want to write a book. I've been dreaming about it for years!" **I tell them all you have to do is write a page a day and every year you can have half-a-dozen small books done -- or one big one.**

Product development is so very important because customers always want something new. If your job is to re-sell to your old customers again and again (which it is), you'd better be creating new items -- or at least, items that have the appearance of being new. One of the things we've done at M.O.R.E., Inc. is to constantly recycle the same materials over and over again. **So it looks like we're cranking out tons of new stuff, but all we're doing is pulling up the same old files and putting facelifts on them**. Now, it's always different, at least to some extent -- but many times it's basically the same message. Every time you get it with a different slant or a different twist, you learn more; you get more.

I'll be specific: every one of the products and programs we sell contains the same basic start-up manual. Why? **Because when people spend hundreds or even thousands of dollars for the program, they expect a nice, big, thick start-up manual.** However, most people never read the damn thing. If they do read it, it's only the chapter that shows them how to get started, which is just 30 pages out of a 500-page manual. The rest of those 500 pages are the same pages we put in every one of our projects. Even if the customers realized that, they still wouldn't care; when they spend a few hundred dollars, they want to see you kill some trees. They want some bulk; they want something that's heavy in the mail. Even if you're just selling them web products, they still want something they can stick on their bookshelf to show they received something for their money. So we just keep selling people the same things over and over again, with new twists. It makes product development quick and easy; it might take just a few days to produce that manual. **People want things that are different or**

sound new, but they want some solidity to them also -- so you keep finding things that are proven, that really work, and you just keep giving them facelifts.

Even if you have customers that know they're buying the same stuff over and over, essentially if they're buying basic, solid information that has a different twist or a different spin each time -- well, maybe the next one they buy is the one they actually sit down with, listen to or read, and comprehend. What people in the opportunity market want is not information -- they really don't, and I know this is going to sound like I'm cynical, but it's the truth. **There are exceptions, but what most people in the opportunity market want is simply a turnkey distributorship of some type, an opportunity where you've already put everything together for them.** They don't want to learn anything; they don't give a damn about that, so if you're going to teach them anything, you've got to sneak it in on them. **They want a product that promises them they can pull it right out of the box, do a few very simple steps that aren't going to take much time, and have something extremely simple that's been proven to make a lot of money.** The more you can do for them, the higher your sales are going to be.

Let me re-emphasize that there are exceptions to this, thank goodness. There are people in the opportunity market who are willing to work their tails off and learn what it really takes to make millions of dollars. But most people in the opportunity market are lazy. They'll admit it if you ask them. **They want you to do everything for them; they just want to collect the check every month.** I have people admit this to me at seminars all the time. I mean, they'll laugh about it -- it's a joke to them. If you can't handle that, then you can't handle the opportunity market. When I get together privately with my best customers, they'll make jokes about the fact that they want us to do everything for them, while they sit back and do as little as possible and collect the most money possible. Don't believe me? You'll eventually find out if you

---

get really involved in this market.

You must develop opportunities that are as turnkey as possible, as simple as possible. So when I talk about product development, I'm talking about turnkey opportunities that give people a product to sell things, the sales material to sell those things, and some kind of a system for selling that allows them to do as little as possible and still get the largest amount of return for the smallest amount of investment in time, money, and effort.

When it comes to product development in the opportunity market, there are two basic categories. **There's what we call the soft product and the hard product.** The radio program this book is based on is a soft product. It's information-based; it's designed to teach people something. Some soft products are motivational, some are educational, and some are a little of both. A hard product, on the other hand, is a turnkey product. It's a distributorship or a master distributorship start-up manual that contains sample copies of the sales material and information about the product to be sold (which in many cases is an information-based soft product), as well as suggestions on how to market it.

When it comes to soft products, keep in mind that you can still sell them to the opportunity market all day long, even though they don't want to learn anything. You sneak it in to them, eventually maybe a switch will flick, and they'll get a little serious. **Usually, what they want is a hard product like I've described earlier. It needs to include a marketing scheme to sell that product or service <u>and the more revolutionary you can make that marketing scheme, the hotter your sales are going to be</u>.** They're always looking for some edge to help them make a fortune -- so give it to them.

Here's an example that's worked well for my friend Mike Lamb. What he's done is create a radio book, an audio book that plays on Internet radio, to further promote and help build his brand. He calls it his Listening Partner Book and people pay him to be allowed to go out and promote and give away the proprietary player that people download to their computer desktop. Then they can download and open up the book for free. Every time somebody gives away the player and finds a new listener, if that listener buys anything, they actually get a commission on whatever's sold. **This is very illustrative of the types of products and services that sell the best in this market.** All Mike's listening partners have to do is give out this desktop icon that Mike created and then the listening partner gets half the money they bring in, forever.

All these people have to do is take one basic step and, from that point forward, they have the potential to make lots of money. **Now, you can't make them a promise or guarantee that they'll profit because you'll go to jail if you do that.** But Mike's listening partners have the potential to make huge sums of money on an ongoing basis and all they have to do is take that one little step. People in the opportunity market go crazy over that general theme of residual income. They love anything that promises residual income, they love anything that promises passive income, they love things that offer huge profit margins. They buy licensing rights packages, they buy websites, and they buy Internet services. **They'll buy all kinds of services related to every opportunity you sell**. Anything that's associated with the product that's being sold, the marketing scheme that you've created to sell it with, and all the tools that go along it, they'll buy like crazy.

Another thing that they buy is what we call a two-tiered distributorship. This is where we bring people in as distributors. Sometimes we give the distributorships away for free; sometimes we make the customers attend a tele-seminar we'll charge a couple of hundred dollars for and then we'll appoint them as distributors -- sometimes for a low fee, sometimes for free.

CHAPTER FIVE

As distributors, they get so much money on the sale of whatever product or service is part of that turnkey program. It's usually a very small percentage; that's the bad news for them. The good news is that our requested entry fee is very small. Then, we send them their distributor kit. **Once we appoint them at that bottom level, we've got them.** Now they're serious, they're distributors, they're representatives -- and then we come along and we tell them, "Thank you for being a representative or a distributor. Now, you're going to get 20-25% of the money you make per sale of this product or service. If you would like to keep more money on every transaction, here's your opportunity to become a master distributor."

The conversion level is high because they're already distributors or representatives -- so now it's easy to ask them to shell out hundreds or, in some cases, thousands more dollars for those higher-end opportunities. You've appointed them as distributors, so now they take it more seriously; so what starts out being something you sell for a few hundred dollars becomes a very easy up-sell.

Now, I know I'm spending a lot of time on product development, but this is a very important element in your success as an opportunity marketer. Having told you what you should do to be profitable, I'm now going to tell you what you shouldn't do. **The most vital thing is this: don't spend that much time on product development. It's not that important to the customer.** Again, at the risk of sounding cynical or disrespectful, they're very lazy people. But that's okay. They know it, you know it, and we're all in it together.

At a seminar I'll say, "Who here in this crowd wants us to do all the work for you, while you sit back and do nothing and get a huge check?" and they all start jumping up and down and cheering. That's the opportunity market for you, like it or not. **If they weren't lazy, they wouldn't buy all this stuff. If they were** true entrepreneurs, they'd be out there doing their own thing. They wouldn't be buying these turnkey programs that promise to put everything together for them; they'd be out there creating their own stuff. That's what my most successful distributors all do. They break away from our company after they use us as a stepping stone to help them get started. As soon as they gain the confidence and knowledge and experience they need, they start developing their own products and services and they're gone. The rest of my customers aren't true entrepreneurs. They just want to get rich by doing the minimum amount of work possible.

So what do people need to spend time on to be profitable in the opportunity market? The sales material, the start-up manual, and the actual products that are sold as part of the turnkey program. Every single turnkey program has to have those three elements. The more bells and whistles you can put in the message contained in the start-up manual, the better. It needs to sound exciting. This approach is significantly different than the way traditional marketers approach their customers. **If our customers really cared about the materials that we send them, we would spend a lot more time preparing them -- but they don't.** Back 10-15 years ago, I thought it all had to be perfect. But then I found out the customers don't care.

We're all in business to serve customers, so you have to give them exactly what they want -- and I'm telling you, your customers in the opportunity market just couldn't give a damn about most of the instructive material you send them. **It's going to end up on the shelf because they want you to do all the work and they don't care about your tips and tricks on how to maximize your profit.** If they actually have to do any work, it may as well be written in Greek because, frankly, they're going to blow it off. To think that this is a marketplace that's made up of business people is ridiculous; they're consumers and, in most cases, they're not entrepreneurs in any way, shape, or form.

A lot of the marketers I know don't understand this. Some of the sharpest marketers I've met -- some of whom have made me millions -- are broke now because they don't understand it. They think they're going to help make people money and that's a nice, high-level concept -- but they think they can help anyone make money. I believe it's foolish to think so because you don't have that kind of power. **You can help them do it and show them all the tips and tricks if they're willing to work hard, but if they'd rather sit in front of the TV and let you do all the work, they're not going to get wealthy.** You can't give them everything. You do what you can, but there are many things you can't do. A lot of people are going to screw it up no matter what you do. You can give them a map and tell them where the gold mine is and all they're going to do is sit around saying things like, "Well, how do I get the shovels? How do I get there? I don't have a way." It doesn't occur to them that they have to put in a little effort to find a way.

I hope you, the reader, aren't this way. I'll be honest with you: while I may sound cynical, I don't mean to be. Yet it ticks me off that more of these people don't do anything. I'm very upset about that at times, but the reality is that I don't worry about it like I used to. There's no point. **Some of my customers will make good money with our programs, but some aren't going to make a cent and they're going to blame us for it.** They'll say that we cheated them. That used to just drive me crazy, but nowadays I'm just more calloused about the whole thing. I've come to the conclusion that some people misplace the map I give them, or the map gets destroyed inadvertently, and they don't know what to do after that. What they really want instead of a map is for you to just pull up in front of their house in a limousine and unload the cash.

I used to be one of those people that wanted everything without doing a lot of the work. I just wanted to be a millionaire 25 years ago, that's all I wanted. **I didn't realize I was going to have to kill myself for it, to work my tail off and learn a whole**

bunch of new skills that were going to be frustrating and time-consuming and emotionally painful. I just wanted the millions of dollars myself, so I understand exactly how they feel. But you know what? As far as I know, nobody makes millions without paying a tremendous price for it. There's a lot of delusion in the opportunity market and I'd tell my customers to wake up and be willing to work a lot harder than they are. The basic business is pretty simple, but that doesn't mean it's easy; learning some of the skills necessary to make a lot of money will cause some real pain, especially during the initial learning curve.

When you look at all the little things you have to do to put a direct mail piece together, you'll see that it's not necessarily a huge undertaking -- but you have to pay attention to what you're doing and it's very time consuming. It's a skill that takes years to develop. My friend Mike Lamb has a keychain his wife got him 15 years ago and it says "Whatever it takes." That's what real entrepreneurs do -- within the limits of the law, of course! **The people who don't make any money just aren't willing to do whatever it takes.** That may be the essence of what I'm teaching you here: Whatever it takes. Don't think about this as a short-term situation; don't think of this as something else you have to do; don't think of this as something like a job. Think of this as an integral part of who you are, of your basic makeup.

If you want to have a better lifestyle, if you want to be able to put food on the table for your kids, if you want to have a legacy to leave behind, if you want to create something, if you want to have employees and be responsible for other people, or just be responsible for yourself, then you have to be the driving force. I don't look at this as a job. I wake up in the morning, I go to bed at night, and everything that I'm doing is all part of my business. It's more like a lifestyle than a job. It's a part of who I am. **I've come to realize that being a business owner is like being a farmer. It's a lifestyle; there's no time clock to punch any more.**

The business tends to be all encompassing. When you look at it that way, you tend to do more and commit more of your time and energy and more of you to the business.

Secret N

This secret involves testing many, many things. You're always asking what's next. One of the heartbreaking things about this market is that it's a lot smaller than you might think. If you want to make millions of dollars in this market, you're going to go through opportunities more quickly. For instance, I've got a friend of mine in Birmingham, Alabama, who's been running the same ad virtually unchanged for 25 years. Every few years he'll give it a little facelift, but it's the same damn promotion it ever was. Because he's running a small little ad, it doesn't cost a lot of money and it's a little promotion that's what I call evergreen. **He can run that little ad forever -- his kids can be running that ad 25-30 years from now -- and it'll still make money because it's a small ad.** You don't need a lot of sales to make a nice little profit on it, especially if it runs in enough publications. Over the last 25 years he's become a multi-millionaire, so he's happy.

But if you really want to go for the gold, you can't just run small ads. You have to run big, giant, full-page ads. **You have to mail millions of pieces of direct mail -- and the one thing you're going to find out real quick is that the market is limited.** The promotions fizzle out after a while. The first time this happened to me, it broke my heart; I was depressed for 6-8 months. The market does replenish itself a little, but not fast enough to keep up with you when you're trying to do something in a major way. So you've got to keep coming up with new stuff, especially if you want to re-sell to your old customers again and again to maximize your profitability.

At M.O.R.E., Inc., we're constantly testing, we're

constantly tweaking, and we're constantly looking for new angles. We model what other people do. We take the things that work for them, and that might work for us, and we test them.

You develop confidence and experience along the way and with that confidence comes the ability to test even more things because now it becomes more enjoyable. The longer you play the game, the more you'll realize that some of the things that scare the hell out of some people will excite others. So now you want to find out what you can do and how many different ways you can re-package things. It becomes a game to see how many different ways you can create new stuff out of the old. **You're constantly looking for ways to give it the appearance of new material, to put new twists on it, but it's really just the same old stuff over and over again.** You're just finding ways to make it look new and fresh and exciting and different.

My best example goes back to the world of rock 'n roll music. One of my favorite bands is Rush, the three-piece band out of Canada. All their songs -- or at least all their songs for the last 20 years -- are pretty much the same. **They follow a theme and there's a range that they stay within; some rock 'n roll bands stay within an even smaller range than that, where the same chords used in every one of their songs sound the same**. Your customers want that, too. Sure, they want new, new, new. You'll always need something new to offer them because that's the way you get the most profit. It's just like the way a band will come out with a new album or new concert: there's always something new in the mix -- and yet it's really just the same thing with the same recurring themes stamped out so they look a little different each time.

You need a certain amount of familiarity to make it comfortable for people to re-buy, but there's got to be a certain amount of buzz that makes it a bit more enticing for them to pay more attention to these new things that you come up with. As long as it sounds new, as long as it sounds exciting, you'll do well.

We've seen what the future is and it's the computer. All the things that we want someone to do, they're going to funnel through the desktop of their computer. That's the theme for this year -- but next year there may be some new theme. **It's always got to be something and it's got to sound revolutionary.** I'm not saying that the computer angle is overhyped, but ironically, the programs that sold best have been the ones with the most hype. They've even outsold the programs that were more solid and based on proven methods; in fact, those solid programs often sell the least.

To me, there's no greater irony than to see a program out there that's earning people millions of dollars, when I know it's pure crap. But it sounds exciting and interesting, so their sales are sky high. Then I see other people selling stuff that's really based on something solid and proven, that has some real value, and those people struggle along. It's nice to come up with a little bit of both -- to have something that's proven, but make sure there's enough hype in there so that the cash registers keep on ringing. **I think you need that excitement to drive someone to pay attention to what you're doing.** You need that sizzle to get them in the door, so they'll take some time to take a look at what it is you've put time and effort into, what your plan is.

It's all a part of your scheme -- and let's take a little diversion to explain that word a bit. "Scheme" is a word like "manipulation"; whether it's negative or positive depends on how it's used. The first time we got called to the Kansas Attorney General's office so that they could meet with us and find out who we were, we were sitting in the Office of Consumer Affairs and they were saying something about our scheme and my little wife popped up and she said, "We don't sell schemes!" They said, "Look, we didn't mean scam." They started backing down from her

-- I mean, here's this little bitty gal, a hundred pounds soaking wet, and they were saying quickly, "Sorry, ma'am, we didn't mean scam!" **Sure, there are regulatory issues in this market you have to pay attention to, but they're nothing to be scared of, nothing to keep you out of the market.**

You need to have your earnings disclaimer -- that's vital. You need to have your terms of service and you need to have your privacy policy. All this needs to be stated explicitly, so when anyone comes to your website or really reads your materials they know what's going on. **It's all in the fine print that nobody reads; it's there for the lawyers and the regulatory police, but it is there. It has to be because in this day and age everybody has to know what's what.** If you're walking up to a line, you have to know where the line is.

Some of the best legal disclaimer language can be stated in ways that are friendly and folksy and sincere. It's funny to me how, the more we practice this, the more we find ways to disclaim all our stuff without using a whole lot of legalistic mumbo-jumbo. **We just tell people straight out what they're getting.** We use language like, "Look, we're not promising that you're going to become a millionaire or make any specific sum of money -- or any money at all. You do understand that, right? Now, let me tell you why this has the potential to make a lot of money." There are ways you can do this that will be less scary than normal.

But back to the subject of testing! You've constantly got to try as many different things as you can, watching the numbers closely and letting the customers vote with their checkbooks and credit cards to tell you what they like the most. **Then you take your bestselling items and pump more money back into the areas that customers want the most.** That's where the sales are. Now, what works best varies with the promotion, but what I mostly look for are the themes that I know, from past experience, the

---

CHAPTER FIVE

customers get the most excited about.

One of the things we're doing right now is simply taking something we started on seven years ago and giving it a facelift. **We're heavily involved now in the world of viral marketing -- what we call chain reaction marketing -- where customers can give stuff away for free.** Other people can pass it along and keep passing it along, just like a snowball rolling down a mountain. A thousand people can give it to a thousand more who can give it to a thousand more and then our customers have these links that are embedded into free e-books so the business can just keep coming back forever. It's those themes that we look for.

More than anything else, though, doing well with testing involves having something that offers the promise and the potential of easy money that can keep rolling in forever, that residual income that gives the customer the chance to make the most money for the least amount of effort and expense. Those things probably affect the overall health of the company more than any other single factor, period. We try to find as many ways as possible to incorporate and re-incorporate as many of those elements into every new promotion that we have.

How you test can be very important. We used to test every week, as part of our weekly new customer acquisition mailing, but that got frustrating and unprofitable, so we stopped that. Our marketing plan is very simple and effective, so now we just test things to our best customers. Then we take the hottest items that get the best response and we test them to the outside list, for new customer acquisition. **That's how we find the promotions that work the best for us: by using established customers as guinea pigs.** If our established customers -- who love us, trust us, feel bonded and connected to us -- won't buy something, if we can't make tons of money from them, then we know we're never going to attract new customers with that promotion.

Don't worry about overwhelming your existing customers, they want to hear from you. I spent years worrying that I was going to try to sell too much stuff to our customers, that they were going get ticked off because they heard from us too much. It doesn't really work that way. Now I worry that I'm not selling to them enough.

Today, I have a mindset that I need to create more products and make more offers for these people or at least do more joint ventures with people. These customers have an insatiable demand for new stuff. That's the thing I didn't realize at first, even as recently as 5 years ago. **The customers are insatiable.** Our best customers are like drug addicts; no matter how much they pump into their veins or sniff up their noses or drink, they just can't get enough. **Dan Kennedy says that consumption expands with usage; the more people get, the more they want. The more they buy, the more they want to buy.**

I think part of the reason I'm successful is that other people aren't making enough offers to my customers. At the same time, I'm a big believer in abundance. In one way I'm grateful that more opportunity people out there don't do this -- but it's a great situation that you, the reader, should take advantage of if you want to make plenty of money. I honestly don't believe that the extra competition will hurt us. **Our methods have served us well in a market well-populated by fly-by-nighters, constantly chasing new customers, because they're not doing nearly enough to develop relationships with the customers they have.** If you do that, you can sell them a huge amount of stuff on the back end.

<u>**Consumption expands with usage**</u>. If that's the case, then the more companies that come into the market, the bigger the market becomes. It really does work like that, in my experience, although the opportunity market is smaller now than it used to be, back when I entered it in the late 1980s. It can be that way again.

Secret O

Our next secret is, simply enough, passion. **You've got to fall in love with the business.** Once I got started, I became 100% obsessed with the business in every way. It dominated every waking moment of my life, year after year -- and along the way, it's made us millions of dollars. It's an easy business to fall in love with because it's just so exciting. **That's one thing I want to convey to you here: it's amazing to get involved in a marketplace that's as lucrative as the opportunity market, where people habitually spend thousands and tens of thousands of dollars just to get the right opportunity.** It's a business you can easily fall in love with. That's large part of the secret of our success.

For years I just wanted to be a millionaire; that's all I thought about. Yet when we finally did start making millions of dollars, I got depressed. I guess I had some crazy idea that once the money started coming in, it was going to change certain things -- but it didn't, really. Since then I've fallen in love with the acquisition of the money: the hunt, the chase, the idea of making a game out of it. In this mindset, you use money as a way of keeping score. **It's a great game; you get an idea and you throw it at your best customers. If they love it, they send you hundreds of thousands or even millions of dollars in a relatively short period of time -- and it's such an awesome feeling.** Now, it's nice to have a good home and a good car and go on long vacations. But nothing compares to the thrill of waking up one morning, having an idea, and finding a way to make money with it. As long as you're testing it to your very best customers first, you're never going to lose. We're doubly efficient that way because we use direct mail to reach out to our customers. We're able to take an idea that we get on the 1st of the month and turn it into hundreds of thousands of dollars by the end of the month.

Every morning I get up and drink a couple of pots of coffee and brainstorm. I'm always taking notes, I'm always thinking of new ideas. Then we have a meeting every single week where we get together with senior staff, along with representatives from our printer and mailing house. All these people have a deep understanding of our business and those meetings are where we actually plan all the mailings and develop the strategies we're working on to go out there with.

We have a strong system within the business and the weekly meetings force us, on a regular and consistent basis, to deal with the important questions: "What are we doing next month? Where's the income we want this month and next month going to come from?" We're constantly planning new mailings all the time and using that as a springboard to take care of all of the implementation.

Now, we have our mailing house and printer there because we schedule our mailings carefully. The mailing house has to work with our staff to get the right list we're mailing that piece to and just having them there, rather than taking care of it on the telephone, lets us solidify our relationships. **It's fine to do business with people you never meet, but it's also nice to have people that are part of your regular team, that you're eyeball-to-eyeball, belly-to belly with on a regular basis.** Relationships get developed, communication is solid, systems get put in place that strengthen over time. What we're all trying to do is turn our businesses into moneymaking machines. The way we do that is by developing good, capable, competent people who can implement all of these wild ideas we come up with.

At our weekly meetings the manager who's in charge of customer service is there because he's got to be able to communicate all these ideas throughout our company -- so when customers call up to ask questions, we've got answers for them. It helps to keep the machine running; it's just like taking a car in and having the oil changed and your tires rotated on a regular basis.

The people in our meetings are also offering ideas; as we brainstorm, they have input. And they've got incentive, too, because we've got a bonus that pays them a percentage of the gross sales that come in. It was one of the smartest things my wife did before she stepped down; now the employees are all "incentivized." When the business is doing well, they're doing well; when the business is doing bad, they do bad. They're the ones helping us shape our ideas. They're the ones constantly saying, "Hey! Wait a minute, T.J., what about this, what about that?" They play an intricate role in helping take these wild and crazy ideas that mostly originate from me and my marketing director, Chris Lakey, and turning them into reality. There's no substitute for falling in love with the business and being passionate about it, seeing it as more than just the money. **It's not just about some way to get rich or to suck money out of customers; it's a game, it's a lifestyle, it's something to put your whole heart and soul into.**

It's such a creative, fun way to make money: art, science, war, sports, with a little bit of politics thrown in there now and then. Passion obviously is a heavy driver.

Secret P

This leads us into the next big secret, which is seminars, tele-seminars, audio programs -- all ways you can bond with the audience. Now, I see so many people who are attracted to direct response marketing who are in love with the idea of getting cash, checks, money orders, and credit card authorizations from around the country. They love the idea that they can stay home and do business nationwide or worldwide. **I see a lot of Internet** marketers, especially, who are in love with the idea that they can sit around and play with their computer all day and get all this e-commerce coming in -- **but the dark side is that too many of the same people just want to put a wall up between them and the customer.** They want to do business with people they never have to talk to; they want to handle everything with email; they want to hide out.

I understand this. The people attracted to this business are those who like spending a lot of time by themselves. **But the best advice I can give people like that is to get to know their customers intimately; that's the way you're going to make the real money.** You have to understand your customers better than they even understand themselves; to know them in such a deep way that you can develop the precise products or services they want. There's no better way to do that on a regular basis than getting in front of the customers, meeting them, looking at them eyeball-to-eyeball. **There's no substitute for interaction with people, even if it's something you hate doing.** It's an absolute necessity when it comes to understanding the customers in the most intimate way, so that you can sell them the most amount of stuff for the most profit.

These entrepreneurs who want to avoid people are really missing the boat when it comes to audio programs. They don't really accept that audio is a great medium for people to get a feeling for who you are, but it is -- because you can be there in front of them without actually being there. You can be there in front of them at their convenience, even in their cars. **They always want to be listening to something new. So if you send a lot of audio stuff out to your customers, chances are good they'll listen to you while they're driving or while they're doing other things that are relaxing and enjoyable to them.** You'll develop a relationship with them through audio programs that you just can't do through print.

While there are writers who can connect with people in powerful ways, those writers tend to be extremely talented -- and that takes a lot of time and years to learn. What doesn't take time to learn, what can be mastered quite easily, is the ability to communicate to people through audio products, where you're expressing an essence of who you are. **All you're really trying to do is keep your heart in the right place. You're trying to help people, trying to reach out, so they'll forgive you for not being professional.** You don't have to be a polished, professional speaker. What you have to do is be totally focused on really trying to help them, reaching out to them, trying to give them more of what they want. Your customers will bond with you in the most incredible ways when you send out audio programs to them on a very regular basis.

My friend Mike Lamb, who's a professional broadcaster, knows more than most that radio is theatre of the mind. **It's a one-on-one communication with somebody, whether he's a truck driver driving down the street listening to the radio and hearing the DJ play his favorite songs, an office worker listening to a talk show host who's trying to raise their ire, or just someone listening to another person sharing their opinion.** Many of us listen at work because it helps make the day go by faster and more pleasantly. Bonding happens and radio stations can turn into multi-billion dollar businesses over the years.

But now anybody can take the same concept and build an audio program into their business. **I think people know when you're talking from the heart, when you're talking sincerely, and when you have a genuine approach to the message you're promoting.** By the time you meet them in person, they already feel that they know you. They've already spent hours listening to you; the ice is broken, the trust is developed. They know you're trying to reach out and help them and they get a sense of who you are.

I believe you should share your personal stories with those

customers. Don't be afraid to tell them who you are, to talk about your struggles and your adversities, to discuss some of the painful lessons that you've gone through. In some cases you may shock people by telling them things about yourself that other people would never dare tell them. <u>You shock them by being so honest; they never forget that.</u> I see so many people who are holding back; they're trying to be professional, trying to be so very polished and perfect, and they think that's the way you have to communicate with people. They don't realize that it's not what people want. **What they want is a relationship with somebody who's just like them, somebody who understands them and their problems and pain, somebody who's trying to help them get what they really want.** That's more important than being perfect and polished.

Those people are too cautious about every word that comes out of their mouths because they're afraid of offending people. So they become lukewarm. Nobody really pays that much attention to them, they never stand out in the minds and hearts of customers, and they never develop strong bonds with them. **The way to do that is to simply take off all the filters, express yourself in the fullest possible way, and show the customers in as many ways as possible that you really do care about them, that you're committed to them.** And be honest with your customers: tell them, "Look, I do want to make money here, but I want to make my money by serving you in the highest way." People will respect that. Those are the things we've done that have allowed us to keep doing business with the same people year after year. They keep coming back and spending more money because they trust us, and there's a genuine relationship there.

Anyone who's been to any of our recent seminars has seen this. Some people talk about how they've been involved with us for years and how they've spent thousands of dollars with us. It's amazing to me how powerful these relationships are that we have with our customers. **It has a lot to do with the fact that we've**

always told our story honestly. The customers know we've struggled with the same problems and confusions and frustrations that they've had; they see themselves in us, as they should. I was out there flat broke for a number of years -- just dirt poor. I could barely put a roof over my head and yet I was sending away for all these crazy get-rich plans and programs. That's the way a lot of my customers are, too. They're struggling so much financially and yet they have an obsession, just like I did back in the 1980s.

Now I'm trying to help them along and they know it. They know I'm trying to help them get rich. But the key word in that statement, of course, is "help." We can't do it all for them, no matter how hard we try. Whether they do anything with what I give them -- well, that's another story. We still have lots of customers who have never made any money, who continue to buy from us on a regular basis for whatever reason they have. Maybe they just stick our stuff on the bookcase and never do anything with it at all; maybe they half-heartedly try something, and give up way too soon. **A story we keep hearing over and over again is that someday they're going to get to it, when they finally do quit their day job.** That's a common theme. I think some people actually do this for entertainment purposes, too. Instead of going to the movies, gambling, or taking vacations, they spend their money on information products that they can turn around and read for entertainment. The act of buying satisfies a deep desire they have.

My wife, Eileen, has a similar obsession, God love her. She's got multiple sclerosis and it's a terrible thing, something I wouldn't wish on my worst enemy if I had one. She can't exercise -- and yet she continues to buy all this exercise equipment. We've got a whole houseful of exercise equipment that she's bought because it promises to be simple and easy and painless. It just sits around; she can't really use it because of her condition. But the very act of buying the equipment soothes her -- that, plus all the books that she buys on weight loss and diets. **Again, the act of buying fulfills a deep, emotional need that some people have.** It doesn't matter whether they use what they buy or not; just the fact that they buy it that makes them feel that they're on the right path.

Chapter Six

A-Z Success Formula: Secrets Q-V

In this chapter, I'll discuss Secrets Q-V in my A-Z Success Formula.

Secret Q is maintaining a stable staff. They say it takes money to make money and, in my experience that's very true. At M.O.R.E., Inc, we've invested significantly in the infrastructure of our business. All my friends call me a kingdom builder and, if any of them read this book, they're all going to snicker to themselves because for years I've taken a lot of criticism for that -- as if I had to do this because of my ego! Oh, maybe there is some truth to that, but there's also truth to this: **if you want to make millions of dollars, you better have a certain number of staff members for every thousand customers you bring in because it's a waste of time bringing them in if you can't support and service them**. The whole idea is to attract and retain customers and the ability to retain customers requires infrastructure.

When you're in a market that's as heavily regulated as ours is, you'd better have staff just to try to take care of every little customer service problem and make sure that your customers get treated right because you don't want those little customer service problems to snowball into something big, which could happen if you don't have the staff to follow up, call people back, and do everything right. So maybe my friends are right to accuse me of being a kingdom builder all these years. I also know it's an absolute necessity to our ability to give good customer support and take good care of all of the people we're bringing in.

Early on, we bought a hospital in our town that was up for demolition -- but the town couldn't even come up with the money to do that much. When Eileen and I bought it, we were two young and dumb kids, just 30 and 28. We thought we were getting a great deal because this building offered something like 30,000 square feet -- and we bought that thing for a dollar a square foot. The day we bought it, we thought that was all we'd ever spend on it. Ha! Since then we've put about a million and a half into it -- so the joke was on us because the whole thing was caving in.

It's a beautiful old building, but it was built in 1928 and needed a lot of work. We're very proud of it and we've filled it with a staff of people that have been with us since the early 1990s. **Every year they keep hanging in there: they love our business and they actually love working for us because we're constantly doing new things.** Direct response marketing in general is a fun business. I see it as a very challenging, very creative, very rewarding way to make money.

We've always had a very loose management style; it lends itself to people who don't want to be micro-managed. I've got a general manager now, though. **The important thing is that the employees are still hanging with us.** I don't know why they stay; but we try to treat them right and we pay them well. There's no question that we pay more money than most companies in the area, so if they do think about quitting, all it takes is a little research to realize we're taking good care of them financially. Add to that the fact that we've got an interesting business and we've all learned how to do it together. The core group of us who have been there the longest have worked together for years, creating systems and developing a lot of the ideas that we use daily. When it's all running smooth, which it usually is, it's just a massive profit machine.

I think it's very exciting to watch my staff work. **They're a creative, energetic group of people and they have the discipline to carry out what they need to -- but they also have a lot of fun doing it.** And it's more like a family thing; I actually love most of these people as family and we've got four different married couples who work with us. We've got a mother and daughter who've been with us for six years; their offices are right next to each other. My son works for the company, my son-in-law works for the company, and there are some employees who are related but aren't married. Usually things like that just don't work, yet we've found a way to pull it off.

Secret R

Secret R in our A-to-Z rags-to-riches formula is planning sessions; I touched on this when I talked about meetings. **Having regular ongoing discussions to find out where the next dollar is coming from is a pivotal point of the growth of any business.** We've been doing regular weekly planning meetings now for over 10 years. We get together on a regular basis, number every single mailing, and check it sequentially. We started with Mailing Number 1, and at one recent meeting, we scheduled Mailing Number 4556.

Every week we get together specifically to schedule new mailings. My printer's there; he wants more printing business. The mailing house is there; they need more business, too. And so I'm committed to them, just as they're committed to us. We know that the more we mail, the more money we make. Naturally, we just want to mail more and more stuff because that's the bottom line. I've mentioned several times that I used to worry that I was going to mail too much stuff to the customers, that I was going to tick them all off, and they were all going to stop doing business with us. That used to just keep me up at night: I don't want to make my best customers think they were walking wallets. Well, I don't feel that way anymore. I'm more worried that I'm not doing enough with them because there's an insatiability in the marketplace. **My customers are going to go buy from other people if I don't market to them. We might as well be the ones getting the money, rather than our competitors!** If for no other reason than that, you should be making offers to them as often as you can. We mail to our very best customers at least 50 or 52 times a year. Sometimes it's even more than that; if a customer sends away for a free audio CD or a free report, they might get an additional 20 pieces of mail coming in to try to convert them to buy that particular program.

Again, in our weekly meetings, we spend most of our time scheduling and planning our mailings. As far as looking at the numbers goes, we do that probably once a month because it takes time for the mail to get out there and back, especially if you're using bulk mail. We used to look at it a lot more often, but there wasn't any real reason to. If business starts to go downhill, we'll study the numbers more closely.

We spend most of our time in our meetings looking at the mailings we scheduled the week before, so we can find out where they're at, when they're going out, if we're meeting our deadlines. We also constantly keep a new front-end promotion out there at all times. We've been doing 50,000 pieces a week for a long time, just to bring us new customers. We also have at least 52 different campaigns per year going out to our established customers. As I mentioned a few paragraphs back, many of these are two-step campaigns that are followed up with multiple back-end mailings that go out once people raise their hands. So, at any given time, we'll have a lot of different campaigns in action. This does get complicated, which is why we have our mailing house representative there. All the follow-ups are taken care of for us by the mailing house; it's all systematized.

It's a pretty simple business or at least that's how I see it. Admittedly, we've grown into it -- so maybe some of my confidence is just because we've been doing it for a long time. And business is good right now. We've had times when it hasn't been, so it hasn't all been a bed of roses; there have been some real struggles over the years. **We've paid a stiff price to learn what we're doing, but the longer we do this the more aggressive we are; the less we think about making big decisions, the less we test when we come up with a new idea for a plan or promotion.** We just automatically send it out to our 30,000 best customers all in one bang, without dividing it up to smaller bites. In the past we were more conservative about that, but you let the numbers tell you what you can and you can't do. If you've got all these great customers who are always going to buy from you, then why not just try to get as much mail out to them as possible?

That's how confidence gets developed -- over a period of time. You see all of these entrepreneurs doing wildly aggressive things and you say, "Man, they're nuts!" But most aren't -- they've just been doing it for so long that they know what they can and can't get away with, so they naturally tend to grab attention for bigger and bigger things. It's not that they're being reckless gamblers or anything like that. **On the contrary, they have a track record. They know what makes them money, so they know they can always be more aggressive and turn up the volume.** I see so many entrepreneurs who think they're going to cross that line and blow their companies up. But for every wild and reckless entrepreneur that takes their company into bankruptcy, there are tens of thousands of others who just aren't pushing it hard enough.

An entrepreneur named Brad Antin used to appear at many of our seminars as a speaker -- and he'd just bowl people over. He'd jump up on tables where customers were sitting and yell at the group, **"If you're refunds aren't high enough, you're**

CHAPTER SIX   119

not selling hard enough!" And he's right, too. Here's what I mean: when people brag about how low their refunds are, that just means that they're not getting the money that could be theirs if they were just a little more aggressive, offering more outrageous guarantees that would cause more people to buy. Sure, some of those people will end up asking for their money back, but the amount of money you'll get to keep will be far greater if you're more aggressive.

Secret S

Secret S is our $100,000,000 Roundtable. This innovation started with the times that Eileen, Russ, and I would get together to develop products. We didn't call it joint venturing back then; that name didn't enter our consciousness until 6-7 years ago. We'd just get together to develop products, with Russ at first, and then we started inviting other people to join us: Alan Bechtold, Jeff Gardener, and a few others. **It's the simplest kind of joint venture you can do, where you get together with like-minded businesspeople involved in the same marketplace you're in.** We developed products together where we'd meet on the telephone, do some recording, and maybe add some print material -- certainly the transcripts of the recorded text at least. Then we each sold these products to our own customer bases and kept all of the money, so we didn't have to worry about this or that person paying us. That's how it all started.

Now why aren't more people doing this kind of brainstorming, recording the calls, joint venturing, grouping the way we are? That's a good question and it may have to do with a dark side to joint venturing that nobody talks about -- though anybody who joint ventures on a regular basis knows all about it. It has to do with egos. **Sometimes the most talented, successful people, the ones that who can contribute the most, are the most**

---

difficult to work with. There's a level of ego there that makes it hard for people to work together, especially over long periods of time. Sometimes there's a disagreement, here and there, and sometimes those disagreements develop into feuds. That's human nature; it's going to happen, but I think that's the reason why more people don't joint venture.

People in direct response marketing generally want to be left alone, especially the Internet marketers I've met. **They want to hide out from the rest of the world.** I can relate to that. I enjoy long hours of solitude working by myself, too. One of the reasons I fell in love with this business is because it's a way of selling to millions of people without ever having much contact with them.

A lot of independent entrepreneurs are also freaked out over competitive issues -- which is a joke. You're not competing with your joint venture partners. That partnership is one of the easiest ways I can think of to make money. **You did your part, other people did their parts, then the product is sold, there's a split, and you get a piece of it.** Quite frankly, that's the easiest way to make money on the planet. You work with somebody, sharing the work, then you both go out and promote it and you make money.

Our $100,000,000 Roundtable group is currently 14 members strong. For years we operated with 5 or 6 members and there were advantages and disadvantages to that, just as there are advantages and disadvantages to having 14 members. I'd have to say that bigger is better when it comes to money, simply because you have more choices available to you.

On the other hand, you're always going to make more money with one joint venture partner than with several others combined; not only is it easier to work with some people than others, simply because of how your temperaments and business plans fit together, but different people get "hot" at different times. **I have one joint venture partner who's making me more money than all of the rest of my partners combined right now, but next year he may be off doing something completely different.** So I think having more joint venture partners is definitely a strength when it comes to making money, although it becomes a weakness in the sense that the more you have, the harder the group is to manage.

In some ways, JV partners are like employees. **The relationships you have, what you expect from them, their strengths and weaknesses, and how much work they actually do affects how much money you make.** My best joint venture partners are the ones who put everything together for me, then come to me and say, "T.J., let's mail this out to thirty or forty thousand of your best customers." Those partners are the ones I love to work with because it takes time, effort, and energy to put these things together. With these guys, all I have to do is show up for a tele-seminar or produce a pitch tape or schedule a mailing or make sure the graphic artists touch the print product up and make it a look a little bit better. And then I have other joint venture partners who come to me with ideas that are unfinished and they want me to put it all together for them -- which takes a lot more time and work. All of us only have so many hours in a day and, the older we get, the less energy we have.

People are people. As I've mentioned, the best people, sometimes, are also the worst people. **The ones who are most talented, who have the most to offer you in terms of actually putting money in your pocket, who can consistently bring you huge sums of money -- many times those people also have massive egos.** You have to treat them a certain way and it takes a lot of work just to do that. But even though they may be pushing the envelope a little too much, they often make you the most money, too.

There's more to it than that, of course. Last summer, I was

having a heated debate with somebody and this person was saying, "Look, what do you want, money or friendship?" And I told him, "I want both. Why can't I've both?" A lot of times people don't understand this lifestyle. They accuse you of only caring about the money; it's almost like they want to make you feel guilty about it. Well, why can't you want money and all the other good things, too? Why does it have to be either/or? **I think you can have it all or, at least, a decent quantity of both.** Some people just want you to feel guilty about the fact that your business, your money, is very important to you. But you don't have to give up money to get other things you want.

Our $100,000,000 Roundtable group has produced hundreds of hours of audio programs. We've also reworked a lot of the audio to create print materials, in the same way that the book you're now reading came about. For years, all we did was give up a couple of hours of our time every week and, simply by doing that, we were able to produce hundreds of hours of audio programs that we found many ways to use to make money. Now we're moving into other markets. We started with eBay -- and since none of us really knew much about making money on eBay, we started interviewing all kinds of experts, learning their secrets. Now we're doing it with real estate experts. **There are so many different experts out there, who want to share their expertise, and many have books and products and workshops and seminars they're trying to sell; and so now the group is working together effectively on that topic.** The beautiful thing about working with a group is the fact that it really does let you use that acronym of TEAM, where Together Everyone Achieves More. Better ideas come from people working together and, while it hasn't been perfect, the business rewards can be great.

When you do a joint venture with one person, it's usually a 50-50 split: you both put in the necessary amount of effort and time to develop the product and then you go sell it. Either you make a split on each sale or each person gets the product to sell individually. With our $100,000,000 Roundtable, M.O.R.E., Inc. generally puts the materials together after the recordings, so we're doing most of the work, spending a lot of our money on mailings, production, and postage -- so our split is weighed somewhat more toward us.

All of our joint ventures have been based on three different models. The first one is the best because it's the easiest and simplest; this is where we all get together just to develop information products that discuss some aspect of moneymaking. Most of our products are based on Internet and direct response marketing; we get together to share our best ideas, producing the product as part of these weekly phone calls we've had for years; then each of us has the ownership to that product. **The only rule we have is that we can't undercut each other when it comes to price.** Usually we get together and help each other develop the sales material to sell the products, too. We all just share it, we all own it, we can do whatever the hell we want to do with it, as long as we don't try to undercut our JV partners' price. Otherwise, there are no rules. It's great; it's simple.

Our other joint ventures fall into two other categories. As of this writing, Russ Von Hoelscher is getting ready to do a seminar. In this kind of situation, 50% of everything sold at that seminar goes to the seminar promoter; so if we all go to Dallas to do Jeff Gardner's seminar, we give him 50% of what we make. If, on the other hand, it's based on direct mail, the rate is 50% after expenses and the expenses are simple: the printing, postage, and production cost for any audio product, that's it. The only thing that complicates it is jealousy amongst certain members. Some people have this crazy idea about competition that I think is so limiting. I scratch my head and try to figure it out because I'm genuinely confused.

I don't really think about competition at all and yet, some

people are obsessed with it. They just can't get over the idea that one person's going to take their slice of the pie...but our market doesn't usually work that way. The pie just isn't limited in size. **There's enough money out there for everybody and, if you can learn from somebody else, it's going to help you do something great or make more money in the future -- so why wouldn't you want to have an association with that person?** People who are overly conscious of the competition, who are very egotistical, tend to be people who have other issues hiding behind all that ego. It's just a cover-up for low feelings of self esteem, so those people tend to cause the most unhappiness in life in general. It's those people who feel good about themselves in a well-rounded way who are the easiest people to work with.

I've met a lot of talented people who are just pains in the ass to deal with. They blame other people for their lot in life. If you're like that (and if you can actually see it), you need to go pick up a copy of Jack Canfield's book The Success Principles. If you do nothing else, read the first chapter. It tells you to take 100% responsibility for everything that you do and everything you are because, at any time, no matter where you are, no matter who you are, no matter what you've done, no matter what you're doing -- you can make a change. **If nothing else, change your reaction to what's happening to you**.

I know how this works. I've gotten so irritated at people in the past because of something that would happen on a Friday afternoon that the entire weekend would be ruined because I was stewing in my anger. Monday morning, I'd be even more ticked off than I was Friday night -- and I'd lost a whole damn weekend.

Here's an example. About eighteen months ago, I got so angry at one of my employees because they embezzled $30,000 that I slammed my hand down on the counter at work. My hand still hurts -- but it's good. Maybe I should go to the doctor, sure, but the pain reminds me that this is what anger does to a person. It can just destroy you. I've hurt myself because of my anger and I have to take responsibility for that. It wasn't the embezzler's fault that I did that, at least not directly. Yet I see a lot of egotistical people who are blaming other people for all their problems and they're not happy at all.

Secret T

We're down to Secret T on my A-to-Z Rags to Riches list. This is Dan Kennedy's Platinum Group, an organization Eileen and I were part of for about 6 years. It was a wonderful experience. Dan Kennedy is a marketing genius and he's helped us as very few people have ever been able to do. So let's talk about the concept of this particular roundtable and a little bit more about Dan. You may have heard his name, but may not be aware of the extent of his reach. He's been in marketing for years and he's been involved in practically every infomercial that's come down the pipe.

I first became exposed to Dan Kennedy when I was a subscriber to Gary Halbert's newsletter. Dan worked out a joint venture with Gary where he sent us a copy of one of his books, The Ultimate Sales Letter. I'd never heard of Dan, but I discovered after I got to know him that we both ran in somewhat the same circles. **I read his book, ended up buying some stuff from him, and ended up on his mailing list**. Of course he knew about what we were doing because our ads were plastered all over the opportunity magazines before 1992, when we stopped advertising in magazines. Until then, every time you picked up any kind of an opportunity magazine, we had a full page ad running in it.

Later, we started doing a bunch of business with him, and then we started consulting with him, driving out to Phoenix, spending good quality time with him, and going to his seminars. When he formed his Platinum Group, he invited us to become members. It was such a rewarding experience. It helped me sharpen my skills and develop my knowledge as a marketer and it helped me move in new directions that I would have never moved in had I not been a part of that group. **Everyone in the group was as committed to success as we are and it helped us in so many ways just to be around them.** We learned new marketing strategies; all of the members of our group freely traded information since that was part of our commitment to the group. You couldn't be a member unless you were willing to reveal all of your secrets and to discuss all of the things that were working for you, so the other members could profit. The support and guidance from these likeminded people was a tremendous boost.

This is a prime example of how people can form relationships and then take those relationships to new levels. It's more than just the camaraderie of getting together every once in a while and talking on the phone; it's about actually putting your heads together, doing joint ventures, and having long-term relationships that put money in everybody's pocket.

There's a synergy that comes from people freely sharing their best ideas with other entrepreneurs. I think Dan was a genius to put the group together -- but many times we were the ones who were doing the work and he was just mediating it and keeping the whole thing moving in a certain direction. **It became a giant brainstorming session where you would get up and present your best ideas, just like show-and-tell when you were a kid.** We met four times a year and, in every meeting, we were required to bring the best ideas we were working on at that time and do some type of a presentation to the group. **The rest of the members then attacked our ideas, showing us the weak areas we weren't thinking about, but they also gave us support and showed us new ways of thinking about what we were doing.** Then we helped them do the same thing. It was fun; it was creative. It was sometime during that period that my skills as a marketer truly became sharpened and it made me millions of dollars. Sure, it may have cost us $10,000 a year, counting travel expenses and such, but it was a good investment because we made millions of dollars just from our involvement and contribution to the group.

When we got involved in the Platinum Group, the fee was about $5,000 per year. **Of course, the more value Dan proved the group had, the more people wanted in, so the higher the fee got.** I believe it's about $10,000 now, if you can even get in; there's a waiting list. Dan is in a great place: he's got a group of people just begging him to get into his Platinum Group, standing in line with their thousands of dollars in hand, and he just can't let them all in because there's no room -- even though he's raised the number of people he includes. It's still under 20 people, but more people wanted in -- and Dan is in this business to serve his customers and doesn't want to turn anybody down, so he let in a few more members.

When you get together with that many likeminded marketing experts, the excitement level gets to be huge. **The thing that was most exciting and useful was the fact that everybody was there to be brutally honest about all of the aspects of their business, <u>both good and bad.</u>** Since the meetings were closed-door sessions, people were able to reveal certain aspects of their business at a very intimate level -- in terms of how much money they were grossing, how much profit they were making, what their exact expenses were, the biggest struggles and challenges they were facing. <u>It was a chance for entrepreneurs who had already gone where I wanted to go to show me how to get there</u>. There were people in those meetings who had been in business for three or four times longer than I had; they'd already made the kind of money that I wanted to make, had solved the problems that I still had to solve. There were times when I would go to one of those meetings and share my problems with my friends -- and I would leave that meeting a couple of days later knowing the solutions to those problems because my friends were able to give me shortcut tips, tricks, strategies, and moneymaking ideas that I would have never thought up on my own.

Your brain can't help but come up with new ideas when you're sitting there and somebody gives you an inkling about something, somebody else helps it blossom a little, and then you work on it and go home and you're thinking, "My God, if I hadn't gone, I would have never created this product!" That product might ultimately put hundreds of thousands of dollars in your pocket -- or more. **I got some of my greatest ideas while I was sitting in those meetings and, to be 100% truthful here, several of the ideas I got were because I was committed and obligated as a member to sit in that seat for two days or two and a half days.** If I hadn't been obligated, I might not have gone. I can't sit still for two and a half days. I've got to be moving constantly -- but I was forced to sit there in that chair, going crazy. The rest of the members thought I was taking notes on what they were talking about, but what I was really doing was working on all kinds of product ideas. I walked away from some of those meetings with ideas that made us millions, just because I had to sit in a chair for two days. I don't mean to be disrespectful if any of my old Group members ever read this book, but you know, it's impossible for me sit still for two hours, let alone two days. <u>Keep in mind, though, that the Group did for me exactly what it was intended to do: it helped me make a lot of money</u>.

Even if you can't get into Dan's Platinum Group, you can probably still join or create a mastermind group to help you move forward. What you're doing when you put a group of likeminded people together is, you're feeding off of each other; you're sharing ideas and receiving constructive criticism, which is always very helpful. That's why we put together our $100,000,000 Roundtable group. Now, I realize there are some members who don't get anything out of our group. I know that because they'll be in for a year or two and then they drop out, they really don't contribute much, so they don't get much in return. **Those who are the most active get the most out of it, period.** It was the same way with Dan's group. I was one of the ones who got a lot out of that group, I think, because I also tried to contribute heavily. I tried to bring things to the group that would really help people and I tried to help all the members shape their businesses and learn some of the things that we'd learned. You get more out of something when you put more into it. Naturally, some ego is involved here; you want to show-off a little bit to your friends.

By the way, Dan Kennedy has made more people more money than any other person on the planet. **He's worked with more of what he calls "first-generation millionaires," people like me who started with nothing, than anyone in the business.** He's one of the top three mentors who helped Eileen and me make the most money. I'd be doing all of our listeners a disservice if I didn't tell them to go to http://www.dankennedy.com and start buying everything that Dan offers. At least become a member of his inner circle and start subscribing to his newsletter.

Speaking of mentors: I've already mentioned that Russ von Hoelscher was the first person who became a mentor; the second is Dan Kennedy. The third isn't really a single person -- it's a combination of everybody who's been involved with us in our $100,000,000 Roundtable. I look at the $100,000,000 Roundtable as a whole rather than as individual members. **There's something remarkable about interacting regularly with likeminded people who are moving in the same direction that you're moving in, who are going where you want to go; you can learn things from those relationships that can help you make huge sums of money, especially when they've already been where you are.** When you have a relationship with somebody who's already had the problems and figured out the solutions and has made money using certain strategies that you're just starting to use, it's almost like you get to live vicariously through them.

You do all kinds of joint ventures with them, first of all; so that's taking it out of the abstract realm and putting money in your pocket immediately. **When most people think of joint venture they think of one-shot deals, but when you're working with a group of people long-term, after you get done making money on that one deal, you'll like them, they're your friends, you trust them, you respect them, and they feel the same about you.** So naturally it's, "Hey, what can we do next?" So, you do something else and you keep asking "What's next, what's next?" The ideas that come from these kinds of relationships can be amazing.

These people are equally as committed and knowledgeable as you are, they have the experience, and you trust them. There are so many things you can do with joint venture partners that you trust. It opens you up, just like all good relationships. You look at an old married couple; they can finish each other's sentences and they even start to look alike after a while. That's the way it is with all our closest business partners. **They become a part of us and we become a part of them.** Whoever said that business and friendship don't mix doesn't understand that as long as the friendship is centered around the business, then those will be the best friendships you'll ever have in your life.

You have to make sure, too, that any friendship that turns into a business relationship, or vice versa, has a strong degree of sincerity. Honesty is crucial in joint ventures because, if you work with somebody in a such a situation and you get screwed, if something is supposed to be done and it doesn't get done, or you didn't get what you thought you should have gotten, then you're not going to want to do joint ventures with that person again. The word's going to get out and nobody will want to do joint ventures with that person.

Entrepreneurs tend to be people who are very independent and stubborn; they also tend to be egotistical. Some of that egotism is essential, if you're going to go out there and face some of the adversities you have to in order build your business from the ground up. **You've got to have pretty strong feelings about who you are and about your place in the world.** But some entrepreneurs are too egotistical; they're too difficult to work with, they're afraid of competition, they want to keep all of their best secrets to themselves. They don't mind if you share your best secrets with them, but boy, they don't want to give up any of theirs! How can you work long-term with people like that?

There are other reasons people don't take more advantage of joint venturing. I think part of it's fear; they're worried that somebody's going to get one over on them. **People like that have a constant barrier up. Sometimes you can peek over it or crawl over it, <u>but it's always going to be there</u>.** They're fearful that you're going to steal all their ideas, go make all the money, and they're not going to get what they deserve. These people have self esteem problems. They put up the face, if you will, of somebody who's confident and energetic and they're out there making noise and doing business -- but the truth is that they're very sheltered. They're not open to a true long-term, honest, genuine relationship. Now, I've dealt with some self esteem issues myself and I know that part of the benefit of working with a group is that you'll tend to take on things that you might never take on alone. We're moving in some new directions right now where, if it weren't for a few other people who were deeply committed, I would have never moved. I would have been too intimidated; I would have stayed where I was comfortable because, whenever you try something new, you always have to deal with a lot comfort zone issues. **I just can't stress enough how important it is to work with a group of people moving in the same direction that you are.** You'll move forward faster, you'll constantly search for bigger things, and you'll end up helping each other reach your dreams.

The friendships that come out of joint venturing are very important because being an entrepreneur can be a lonely experience -- even if nobody talks about it. We work a lot of hours, and nobody understands us. People around us pity us; they call us workaholics and think we need professional help. **But when you're working with other entrepreneurs, you're working with people who understand you and your problems.** They know how important your business is to you. You're able help them build their business and they're able to do the same for you. The more you do to help them, the more you help yourself.

I think we all have self-esteem issues at certain times in our growth as business people, even if you're the strongest, most socially active, open, energetic person on the planet. You're going to face hesitation and frustration and you have to move through them. I used to have a quote from Dan Kennedy hanging in my office: "Distractions abound; we must fight for focus." I see so many business people, including myself, fighting the distractions. **During my twenty years in business, there have been so many times when I've been anything but focused and I see that as a continual problem with entrepreneurs.** It's a struggle; don't let anybody try to tell you otherwise. No matter how successful people are, I believe that there are always times when they have to fight for focus. You have your good days, you have bad days, you have some days of **struggle. A lot of people think that they're eventually going to get to a place where that ends -- and I just don't believe that happens for most people.** It does get better, though, when the money gets better. Heck, everything does. That's the name of the game.

One of my biggest pet peeves is this book that sold bazillions of copies called Do What You Love and the Money Will Follow; I've mentioned it before. I think it's a joke. Let's get real here: how many butterfly collectors are millionaires because they collected butterflies? None, I'll bet. No, what have to do is fall in

---

love with those few things that bring you the most money. Spend all of your time doing those few things and let everybody else do all the rest. **This concept that you can make money with what you love to do is a great idea, but in the real world you usually can't make money doing those things <u>because the market doesn't allow you to</u>.** I've said it before and I'll repeat it because it's important: what most people love to do is screw off and eat at nice restaurants, stay at nice hotels, get pampered a lot, go drink coffee all day at Starbucks, and go to movies and concerts and cruises. Good luck with that. If you can figure a way to make a lot of money and do all that stuff, great, but it's not likely.

Really making money as an entrepreneur is all about multiple income streams. I heard an acronym several years ago that sums it up, from a book by Michael LeBoeuf called The Perfect Business. **He talked a lot about PIGs, Passive Income Generators. Well, I want to have a whole farm of nothing but PIGs -- and not the kind that slop around in the mud.** To set some of these things in motion, you have to learn from people doing it and then you have to go out and do some trial-and-error yourself. If you have your own ideas and your own ego driving you, you're going to make some mistakes, but an effective entrepreneur learns from those mistakes. Then you come back and decide how much time you're going to put into it. **I know some people who work 20% of the normal work week and make huge amounts of money, while playing the other 80% of the time.** If that's what you want to do, fine; if you feel you've earned that and that's the lifestyle you want, more power to you. With me, it's been a total obsession; I wish I could work a few more hours sometimes, but I can't. There are only so many hours in a week. I'm very, very wrapped up in the business, but I know other people aren't and they're able to make a lot of money and have plenty of leisure time.

A million different people will run their businesses in a

million different ways; there's no one way to do it, but there are guidelines, there are directions you can follow, and lots of food for thought in the way other people are making their money.

Secret U

We're up to constant product development, which is crucial. In my company, there's a constant evolution of ideas and always has been; that's part of our strategy for dominating the market as best we can. So let's talk about how people develop ideas and why it's important to constantly produce new products.

The reasoning is pretty basic: your customers want and demand new things constantly. If you're not giving them new things to fill their needs, they'll go somewhere else. Our customers are insatiable. They want to buy more stuff and they're going to buy more stuff, whether you're selling it to them or your competition is. It might as well be you, right? If there were no other reasons to constantly develop products, that reason alone would be enough. The money's on the table; it's up to you to develop the new products that will put it in your hands. **The ability to do so comes from an intimate knowledge of who those people are and what they want the most, combined with your ability to use that knowledge and turn it around on them.** You're able to develop products that match the mold of what the customers want. The more you do it, the better you get.

Some of our early products are a joke to me now. I only keep them to remind myself of how far we've come and because I want to get a little laugh every now and then. But hey, we were doing our best back then -- and hopefully ten years from now I'll be laughing at some of the stuff we're doing today.

How do you create these products? Work on them a little

every single day. There's just no other way, really; every day you need to be spending an hour or two on nothing but product development. If you'll do that, you'll be amazed at how much you can get done every year. **If you're looking for effective ways to re-package the same stuff, to give things facelifts, you'll always have something new to offer.** It may look brand-spanking new, even if it's just a variation on everything else you've been doing. It's not cheating; a lot of time you just approach the topic from a different angle. You can create multiple themes, using the same basic materials again and again, so you keep coming out with variations that take you very little time to produce. Update old packages. Create deluxe editions that sell for a little more than the original.

Here's an example of something we often do. We've got something called a Joint Ownership Package; it's a special licensing package we sell people that allows them to sell one of our products and services. It's all in the way that we package things. **We have the manual all put together and, while I worked my ass off to produce it, <u>I did it just once</u>.** Now, whenever we want to come out with a Joint Ownership Package, all I've got to do is spend two hours of my time telling my typesetter to change this, change that, change these numbers to this, change this title to that. I call my graphic artist and say, "Change the cover," and that's it. Basically, I built a template that takes very little time to modify. Now, every time I want to sell a Joint Ownership Package, I just make cosmetic changes to the text. These things typically sell for $2,000-$4,000, so it's a nice bit of income that I don't need to work too hard at.

Secret V

Secret V is closely aligned to Secret U: you need to rework your past sales material and promotions continuously. Our customers don't care if a new product is set up using a template, even if they've bought another package and can compare the two side-by-side. After all, despite the similarities, they've got something new, a Joint Ownership in another product or service. They're not really paying for the material anyway; they're paying for the opportunity to represent that particular package. Why re-invent the wheel? **When you've got a system that works, all you're doing is tinkering with internal mechanics.** Remember: customers like things that are new, but they also like it if those new things have a familiar element. They don't want things to be totally new. Nobody wants to be the first one out on the dance floor; nobody wants to be the guinea pig. Your customers want things that are based on proven principles, that have been part of something that's older and more established, because that gives them the feeling of security that they like to have when they buy this stuff.

Let me re-emphasize: you only have to do a little of this every day. It's amazing how this adds up; you can easily have several products in development at the same time. This is especially true when you're doing audio products, like the one this book is based upon. **The customers really don't care if it's all professional and polished, what they want is for you to be real with them, to share secrets that really can help them get where they want to go.** They want usable information. I've produced hundreds of hours worth of audio products that are just me ranting and raving and screaming and howling, but I'm sharing ideas that really do work and I'm giving my customers what I know that they want. So who cares if I stutter and stammer and say things that are politically incorrect or whether I repeat myself constantly? They don't. *What they care about is that I know my stuff, that I care about them, and that I'm honestly trying to give them more than what I promised I would in exchange for the money that they gave me.*

Now, regarding this area of constant product developments:

are there any pitfalls? Sure there are. Earlier in this book, I told you that you shouldn't spend too much time developing your product because it was unnecessary and the customers really don't care that much about that. **What I really meant was that you should spend the majority of your time on the promotional materials that sell your product.**

I have a good friend (whose name I'm not going to mention here) who just spent over one year of his life working on this great product. It really is a dynamite product, quality through and through; it's perfect, a product that he can be proud of for the rest of his life. It was an enormous effort on his part; he sacrificed long hours to put this it together and then I asked him the other day, when he was just finished with it, when he was still exhausted from the effort, "So…did you have a sales letter for it?" And basically he told me he didn't. He had a little bit of copy written for it, but that was it. In my opinion, that's a huge mistake. <u>The majority of your time should be spent developing the sales material</u>.

Quite often, in order to sell the product, you don't want to teach them anything in your sales material, you just want to share the benefits, not the actual features. Or, you want to cover the emotional advantages of the ideas you're sharing rather than the ideas themselves because you want them to spend their money to find out what all the ideas are. Thus, you want to keep it somewhat blind. **By the way, blind advertising really works well in the opportunity market.** A lot of the ads we've written over the years have been blind ads.

For instance, we've got a promotion we're doing right now for this company out of Paramount City. We're promoting their multi-level company called Emerald Passport, but we don't tell people the name of the company in the ad. I've got a six-page sales letter that goes on and on about all these people making

$20,000, $30,000, $50,000, $100,000 a month in this totally new kind of company -- but I never tell them what the hell it is. They're not going to find out, either, until they shell out $500. Part of the reason they're going to be glad to do that is to get the rest of the story.

Chapter Seven

A-Z Success Formula: Secrets W-Z

Secret W in my A-Z Success Formula is joint ventures. I realize I've already talked a lot about JVs, but these points are worth repeating. For anyone just starting out, I think it's vitally important to look for joint venture partners, especially those willing to be long-term rather than short-term partners.

In other words, look for people like Russ von Hoelscher was for us. Look for people doing big things; try to find people who are already where you want to be. Create what I call a "hit list" or "target list." Find fifty or hundred people you want to do business with, who have something to offer you -- and then go after those people. Write them a letter and send them some stuff that you're doing. If you write a new report or produce a new audio CD, send it to them, and don't ask them for anything. **Don't try to solicit business; just try to ask them how you can help them, how you can serve them, and what can you do for them and it's going to set you apart from every other person they hear from.** Don't think that you can't do business with some of these big-name people, because you can. Just realize that you need to proceed slowly and build that sense of trust before trying anything colossal.

What I mean is, don't just come at them and say, "Hey I want to do this, I want to do that, can you do this for me, can you do that for me?" You've got to make them fall in love with you a little bit at a time; you've got to wine them and dine them and tell

---

them you love what they're doing and ask them if there's anything you can do to help. **Show them some of the materials you're creating and offer to let them use your stuff as free bonuses.** <u>That's the way you win people over and I can't give any better advice when it comes to joint venturing</u>. Too many people are looking for one-shot deals; too many of these Internet marketers are trying to hide behind their computers and they never want to talk to anybody. They want to handle everything through electronic mail. I understand that, but I really wonder if they're not missing the boat.

Actually, I know a lot of them are. I appreciate their need to be independent, but the benefits that you get from a joint venture have nothing to do with being dependent on anyone. **It has to do with contributing to the group, trying to do things that really reach out and help their business. <u>It's not just take, take, take, it's give and take</u>.**

Even if you're the independent type who doesn't want to be a part of a group, I think you should try a joint venture at least once. When you actually get a check, then you're turned on to the fact that there are other people that you can duplicate this scenario with. My God, wouldn't it be great if you could have fifty joint ventures a year and make $25,000-30,000 on each one? Well, that's not impossible! We know people who do nothing but joint ventures now; that is, they create products for the sole purpose of doing JVs with others.

There are a lot of people that could be benefiting from joint venturing who aren't. I would just encourage you not to be afraid of the competition; if you're willing to be open and helpful, you can easily work with people who are involved in the same marketplace you're in. We've found a way to make it work. It hasn't been a bed of roses; there have been some struggles and we've had members of our group who ended up hating each other and going to war with each other. **I don't mean to paint an unrealistic picture here; like everything in life, sometimes the best things are also the worst things.** <u>But the advantages far exceed the disadvantages in this case</u>.

And I think it's safe to say that everybody is going to have a bad joint venture here and there. But the good ones are going to far outweigh the bad ones. People ask us all the time, **"Why do you just continue to do business with the same people over and over again?" Well, one of the reasons is that we've had some really bad relationships.** We had a situation like that recently -- a joint venture relationship with a guy out of Atlanta who ended up screwing some of our clients. That's a terrible thing that makes you appreciate your good JV partners a whole lot more; it makes you want to do more business with them instead of going out and finding new partners. It's easy to remain in a comfort zone, especially when there's such a huge payoff. Some comfort zones are good.

Look at my situation with Russ von Hoelscher; I can't think of a better situation. Am I comfortable working with Russ? Hell, yes. I trust the guy, I love him, he's a good friend of mine, he's somebody who's extremely knowledgeable, he's easy to work with, there's a mutual respect and admiration for each other there. It's the most comfortable thing in the world to do business with somebody like that. **So, do I feel that in some ways it's a bad thing to stay with what you're comfortable with? No. It's like a fine wine; it gets better with age.** That's how a good friendship is and it's nice to do business with people you really care about on a personal level.

Those same feelings that make you so connected to those people also make doing business with them a lot more fun. You want to do more business with them because it's part of your social life. When you're working with people, making money with them, then you're able to have a good time with them. I think these are the best social lives for people who are absorbed in their business the way I am. You don't have time for anything but your business, so if you're working with other JV partners who are helping you, and you're helping them, then it really is a win-win situation; and, to me, it offers the best of all things. **More people should look at joint venturing as a friendship deal; you don't need to deal with all the complicated legal crap that a lot of people recommend**. I've done millions of dollars worth of joint venture deals with no contracts, no lawyers, none of the technical BS. It's just done on a handshake -- two friends doing business with each other. If you're friendly, honest, and genuine, you're going to come back and do it again. Joint venture deals can be structured simply and easily and, as long as both parties are keeping it simple and doing what they both say they will, you don't have to worry about getting screwed. And, naturally, when you get past one deal, you start looking for the next.

Secret X

I call this one Operation Money Suck, a term invented by the master copywriter and marketer John Carlton. You might be surprised to learn that this is all about delegation, which I've discussed previously. **Carlton teaches that the whole concept of "money suck" is to focus all your energy and time on those few areas that make you the most money or could, potentially, make you the most money.** Let everything else go; either delegate it or just don't do it.

There are so many things we can do to make money; that's the problem. We have an endless number of choices. You have to fight for focus and it's a never-ending battle, given all the distractions we face every day.

But you need to leverage the maximum number of available hours and energy you have into those few things that could make you the most money. This includes anything that you can do to become a better marketer. Self study, attend seminars and tele-seminars, purchase products, and study advertisements -- anything that will help sharpen your marketing, copywriting, or communications skills is a good thing. Your time should be focused on product development, so you're constantly creating new products for your existing customers and for the people you're trying to attract as part of your new customer acquisition programs. Sure, you'll have some ideas that are more exciting than others and some that are going to make you more money -- but you never know which ideas those are. **Sometimes the things you think are going to be the biggest winners aren't, so you should constantly do everything you can to keep coming up with more new stuff, so that every once in a while you'll hit a grand slam.**

Let me re-emphasize that you need to let other people do all the other work. There are too many distractions in any business and I think the worst thing anybody can do is try to wear all the hats in their business. **The best thing you can do, if you're a marketer, is hire a good manager.** As you grow, you might need a couple of them; but in any case, you need to stay away from the company itself and the day-to-day operations, which are boring anyway, so you can create products and market. Let somebody else do the customer service. Find good, capable, competent people and then spend all your time working on the specific things that can bring you the most customers and keep those existing customers coming back: product development, working on new promotions, working on new ideas, developing copywriting skills.

While I have a pretty sizable staff, I realize there are a lot of people out there who don't -- who work for themselves out of a home office. **Well, you can still delegate much of your work by outsourcing.** For example, with Elance.com, you can find thousands of people willing to do a wide variety of work for you. For example, my good friend Eric Bechtold has been handling everything himself, but he just can't handle the phone calls any more. Well, there's a client of ours who's been coming to our seminars for years and he's looking for opportunities and he's just about there. He just needs a little bit of a leg-up, so Eric's going to start filtering all of his calls through this client, who is very capable.

There are good people everywhere -- you can find them if you look for them. You don't have to hire them as employees although I would suggest at least one good full-time staff person who can handle all of the little things -- the things that take five minutes here, ten minutes there, fifteen minutes here, that when you add them all up together represent a large block of your time, energy, and your focus that could be channeled into something a lot more productive.

Let your staff take care of those little things that distract you from the big picture, even if it's just little stuff like putting letters in the mail, paying bills, or shipping stuff to people. Find somebody who doesn't mind doing all that, someone who's easy to work with, capable, and competent. Let them schedule your phone calls for you, so that when you do get on the phone with people, it's done at pre-arranged times when you're able to block out a bunch of calls together. Look -- most people are constantly putting out brush fires every day because they've been led to believe that you've got to be the first one in the office in the morning and the last one to leave at night. They're working their asses off, putting in tons of hours, and they come home every day exhausted. They're getting old before their time. I used to do that when I was trying to run my company. I would come home tired at night and my wife would say, "What did you do today, T.J?" and it was hard for me to tell her what I'd done. I knew I'd done something -- I'd spent five minutes on this problem, ten minutes on that problem, then somebody else had a problem here that took fifteen minutes…**I was putting out brushfires all day and the company suffered greatly because of it. I wasn't focused on all the things**

necessary to bring in the largest amount of sales and profits.
That's what Operation Money Suck is all about.

Here's another point to consider: the loss of creativity when
you're not focused on the big picture, when you're always dealing
with small things and always taking care of the day-to-day
mechanics. It's easy to do and entrepreneurs love to stay busy.
**They love constant movement -- but you have to school
yourself to remember that the things that you should stay
busiest with are those few things that can potentially bring you
the most money on a long-term basis.**

Are there certain skills that someone needs to have to be
one of the people you delegate to? Of course there are. But it's not
about competency nearly as much as it's about willingness. There
are some people who are willing to do whatever you ask them to. If
you say, "Hey, go down to the store and get me a gallon of orange
juice, will ya?" they'll just go. They're not going to say, "Well, do
you have a couple of dollars? How much is it?" or "What? You
want me to go to the grocery store?" The best people just do it.
**There are some people who, although they're very smart and
capable and competent, also think that a lot of things are
beneath them.** They think they're overqualified to do most of the
stuff you need them to. They're just not easy to work with -- and
they're not going to be around very long, either.

Even those people can have a place in your company as it
grows. But the person you choose to be your assistant needs to be
somebody where you can give them a list of a hundred things and
walk away, knowing they'll handle all of them -- that nothing is
beneath them and that they'll do a good, capable, competent job for
everything you've asked them to so. You'll be amazed to discover
all the little things you have to do -- and when you get them done,
they're not weighing on your brain and taking space in your mind.
You just hand them off.

Now, there's a difference between delegation and abdication. Abdication is when you just hand something to somebody and say, "Look, I don't want to deal with it. You deal with it." Delegation is where you hand it off, but you're constantly overseeing the whole process. **Of course, there are some people who are so competent that they're going to do what you tell them ably and without fault, so with them you can abdicate something, to an extent, knowing it's going to be done and it's going to be done right.** But there are also people who tend to be less reliable -- and again, it's more about attitude than mental capacity. If you were to give me a choice of either a person who has a low I.Q. with a heart of gold who's willing to do anything or some super-smart Mensa genius who thinks he's better than everybody else and is a pain in the ass to work with, then I would much rather choose the former than the latter.

Most entrepreneurs have trouble with delegation because they want to control everything; that's part of the reason we become entrepreneurs. But one of the biggest mistakes we make is that we expect other people to be like we are; we really do. But other people aren't like we are. They're not that driven; they're not that motivated. In order to work with other people, consistently, you can't hold them to the same standards you hold yourself to. And you have to praise them, tell them they're good people and they're doing a great job. **Everybody loves a pat on the back, so you always have to make sure you reinforce those great feelings. If you do, they'll pay more attention to you and they'll do the things you need to have done on a more consistent basis.** Catch them when they're doing things right, give them lots of praise and lots of encouragement, and pay them well.

Some entrepreneurs look at their relationships with employees, joint venture partners, and suppliers as costing them something. What they fail to realize is that if you find the right people to put in those slots, it's almost like an investment towards future profits. Those people will make you money you wouldn't have made without their help. It's very important to be able to hand something to somebody and know that it's going to get done.

Secret Y

You shouldn't be in this business just for yourself; that's my next secret, the second-to-last on this list. You're in it for the company, family, friends, and staff; you should regard people as the most important element of your business because they are.

There's something that never shows up on the profit-and-loss statement; I call it the emotional side of the business. I've surrounded myself with people that, by and large, I really, truly care about; the best examples are my son and my son-in-law. Both work with me on a daily basis and I love both these guys -- and I know that they love me. There are other staff members with whom I also feel very deep emotional connections, especially the ones I've been working with for years. **They're more than just people I work with; they're people I really feel connected to and I enjoy them.** Then there's the emotional connection I feel with joint venture partners I've been working with for years. It's about a whole lot more than just making money -- but here's where the money comes into play.

When you're looking out for people you really care about, and you're trying to serve them and contribute to their lives because they're contributing to yours, you'll come up with ideas for making more money that you would never have come up with had you not had those relationships. Dollars and cents are important, but it's about a hell lot more than just that; it's about people who will spur you on. You'll find yourself doing more because you're committed to these people. This is one of those things that's hard to talk about; I know for sure it doesn't show up in traditional

---

business classes and you won't find it in most books about business, but I also know it's true. **Working with people whom I truly care about and who care about me has made me a lot of money that I would have never made if I'd tried to isolate myself and do everything on my own.**

It's a good idea to look at your best customers in much the same way. I enjoy mine; I enjoy spending time with them and I feel the connection with them. **I get very upset sometimes because I'm really trying to help them and I wish I was able to help them more than I do.** That's one of my biggest frustrations. Sometimes I get frustrated because, although I'm trying my best to help them, either they don't get what I'm doing, they don't understand the value of it, or for some reason I haven't connected with them.

Let's go back to something we talked about earlier. It's not a very attractive idea, but it's reality. Most customers in the opportunity market want to get rich without doing a single thing and they'll even joke and laugh with you about it. I'll go to seminars and hear them whining and complaining and all of a sudden I'll have enough of a connection with them that I'll pat them on the back and say something like, "Hey, John, you just want to get rich without doing a damn thing, don't you?" and then they'll chuckle and say, "Well, yeah." This is part of the insanity of the opportunity market. I was like that myself, once. I had delusions of grandeur and I thought the money was going to come right out of the sky. **But I always had a work ethic; that's the one difference between me and a lot of the customers that I work with.** They're really just looking for something for nothing and I don't mean that as a judgment call. I really care about these people, but by their own admission a lot of them are too lazy to accomplish anything. They want somebody else to do everything for them. In many cases, those are the promotions that worked best for us -- the ones where we promise to do everything for the customers. But they would benefit much, much more by learning some of the things I've been talking about in this book.

Secret Z

This is it! The last secret in my A-Z Rags-to-Riches Success Formula: knowledge and experience equals confidence and wealth. This goes back to that whole myth of the entrepreneurial hero. When Eileen and I did our first seminar, if it hadn't been for Russ von Hoelscher, we never would have made it through. We were like those scared little bunnies that you see in the pet store: they shiver and just want to hide out in the corner. **We were attracted to direct response marketing because we loved the idea that you could do business with people you would never meet and, in most cases, never talk to; as I've mentioned, that's the way most direct response marketers are.** They want to live in their own private, little world and be shut off from everybody and still make great money. Russ is the one who talked us into having seminars. He convinced us that this would be a good move…but we were like scared rabbits and wouldn't even get up on the podium and say 'Hi' to the people because we were too frightened and insecure.

Nowadays, we do three-day seminars without thinking about it. You can't pull me off the stage now. Looking at me, you'd think I was born with the confidence to get up there and perform, but nothing could be farther from the truth. A lot of entrepreneurs are confident, but people don't realize that their confidence was developed over a period of time, with them learning new skills and facing lots of adversity and uncertainty along the way. You get confidence by slaying those dragons. From a physical standpoint, let's say you were to go to the gym and work out for an hour every single day. I guarantee you that, after a while, your body is going to start toughening up. You can't help it -- if you go to the gym and work your tail off every day for an hour, it's only a matter of time before you have a better body. **It's the same way with building a business: you get better, stronger, more capable, more competent, more knowledgeable over time. It all comes, but it comes through a process <u>and that's what the newcomer doesn't realize</u>.** They see these established entrepreneurs and they're intimidated by the level of confidence these people have, without even realizing for one single second that that was all developed over a period of time. I wish somebody had told me that back when I was first getting started.

It's a genuine confidence. You start feeling that you have a lot more power and that means you can use that power in ways you never thought possible. With me it started out with egotism. Now, on the outside, egotistical people can fool you sometimes; if you get around them enough and know the symptoms to look for, you'll see that there's a difference between egotism and true confidence. **Real confidence is something that's developed by getting very, very good at just a few things that produce the largest amounts of revenue for your company.** So, did my confidence move my egotism out of the way? Eventually, yes. And here's what else moved my egotism out of the way: facing a lot of adversity and, to put it bluntly, getting my ass kicked.

Currently, we're starting to getting involved in real estate marketing. We're interviewing a number of real estate experts and recently I was talking to a new speaker who's been helping people make money in real estate for 15 years now. He said to me, "T.J., do people really think they can go to a three-day seminar and learn everything it takes to get rich in real estate?" Well, yes. They do. It's ridiculous to believe that because, in most cases, it takes years to get really good at anything. **But that shouldn't discourage you; as long as you have customers, you don't have to be a perfect marketer to re-sell to your same customers again and again.** These are people who trust you; once the ice is broken, it's easier to resell to them than to hook a new customer. This may seem difficult to pull off, but your abilities and your confidence will grow over a period of time.

There are people who believe they know more than they do. There are people out there who see certain things and think that's all they need. But you've got to have a little bit of humbleness going into a business, knowing that you're not going to learn everything overnight, that you're certainly going to make mistakes, that you're going to lose money. The ultimate thing is to make sure you feel in your heart that if you put good time and effort into something, if you're on the right track, then eventually whatever it is you're doing is going to be a success. Sometimes you've got to find out a few things you don't want before you find out what you do want. **Sometimes you have to test a lot of different things before you finally figure out where your niche is -- and in the opportunity market you will find a certain niche.** The most successful companies in this marketplace have found certain areas they're very comfortable in, so with their programs they just keep re-stamping out the same themes over and over again. You've got to test the water a little -- maybe a lot -- before you find out which direction is best for you.

The moral of this A-to-Z wealth formula is simply this: nobody gets rich by accident or by themselves. **A lot of what I've been trying to share in this book has come from reflection. The ability to reflect takes time and experience, so you can look back and see everything through different eyes.** Sure, obviously some people get lucky right away and achieve great success early on, which can distort their perceptions of how good they are. We made over $10,000,000 in our first four years -- but we also struggled for a number of years before that. It's almost a bad thing for somebody to hit it by accident right out of the gate. That's probably more of a curse than a blessing. I think this is an aspect of the same concept that holds true in the music industry or

---

Hollywood. **When you're a young performer and you get really big really fast, not only can it go to your head, but it can mess up your whole life.**

The money is like a drug, in some ways, because it can be addicting. It can lead to as many bad things as good things. It gives you more choices, so sometimes you make wrong decisions. But hey, the real joy is in the work that you do; it's in the business that you built; it's in the people you work with on a regular basis; it's in all the creativity that comes from developing ideas and turning them into reality. The money is nice, but it's the other things that make it all worthwhile. **I would especially encourage you to go back and reread the sections where I talked about joint venturing and falling in love with the business. All these things do affect the money -- there's no question about it.** Don't fall in love with just the money alone; it's not worth it. You hear about so many people who have all the money in the world, yet they're living miserable lives. They're killing themselves in a thousand different ways.

I honestly believe that the business itself is the most important thing. Business is a game. Finding the right players, the right resources, the right vendor partners, the right elements that will make your business the success you want it to be -- it's all part of the game. The majority of the companies in the opportunity market are, unfortunately, what I call fly-by-night companies. They have no concept of building long-term relationships with customers and getting those customers to come back again and again. **But this is a marketplace where anybody willing to work hard can get rich by following the ideas I share in this book, if only because so few of our competitors are doing it.** There are so many seminar companies that literally blow into a city, generate a seminar, and then blow out of the market and have lousy customer support. They're totally hit-and-run and they give a lot of other companies -- the ones that are genuine, the ones that are sincere, the ones that are out there are doing a good job -- a really bad name.

You find that in every industry, by the way. Look at my friend Ray Prieba, who's in the massage business. He's a serious, dedicated massage therapist; and yet because the name of his company is TLC, he gets every kind of pervert calling him on a weekly basis. They're all looking for an erotic massage. There's sleaziness in every marketplace, companies that are dragging it down, but the opportunity market is especially bad. It's filled with people who don't understand the value of a long-term relationship, so they're trying to make all their money on these initial sales. **In my opinion, the purpose of a sale is to get long-term business. That's where it begins, not where it ends; that's what's made us millions of dollars.** Just practicing that good old-fashioned business, like the kind your great-grandfather used to do, where you're trying to look out for your customers.

I realize that we have customers who don't love us; they're not happy with doing business with us; we're not able to satisfy them. But why do they keep coming back? Well, a lot of them don't. I don't want to try to paint an unrealistic picture here. We've got customers that we've never been able to satisfy and that's fine; we send them on their way and wish them the best. You can't satisfy everybody in any industry. **The point is, we have enough customers who continued to do business with us -- though a lot of those people aren't satisfied entirely either, to be quite honest with you. <u>Part of what drives the opportunity market is this dissatisfaction, period.</u>** A lot of the people in the opportunity market -- I've said this before and it's worth repeating -- are not really entrepreneurs. My friend Mike Lamb calls them "hope hunters"; they're looking for hope. That's not a put down. As the great copywriter Gene Schwartz put it, "What people want is a miracle." And we're trying to find those miracles for them, by constantly learning and constantly reapplying the very ideas that

I've talked about in this book.

Information-selling is the most interesting and exciting business there is. You're creating a wide variety of different products and services that are 100% proprietary and are totally unique. **There are competitors out there, but there's no real competition because, again, this is an extremely rabid market.** These people keep buying and re-buying like crazy and they'll spend huge sums of money doing so. I hope you, the reader, get involved in this marketplace; we need more people willing to do it big and to do it right. Those two things are synonymous in my opinion because doing it big means that you can't just go for those one-shot deals.

New customer acquisition is the hardest thing in this business and people who aren't deeply committed to building relationships with their existing customers are hurting themselves and the field. They're focusing their efforts on trying to do business with people who don't know them, who don't trust them. **They'll get some sales, sure, and maybe turn a little profit, but they're never going to get rich.** To do that, you've got to focus on your back end and relegate your front-end marketing to the status of a necessary evil. Fly-by-night companies put their whole focus on going out there and trying to get new customers to buy their little gizmos; but to a real marketer, that's just a means to an end.

I recently had lunch with a gentleman who's in the business of buying and selling businesses. I found out more about it at lunch than I already knew, but I also shared with him what we're doing. **It was an entirely new world to him; his eyes opened up as we were talking about various elements of it and what can be done -- the E-books and the E-zines and the whole suite of web marketing-related items that we currently use.** It was literally an eye-opener for him to discover that this market actually existed to the extent that it does -- and that it can earn you a huge amount of money. If you can develop a good understanding of the insatiability of this marketplace, and learn how to keep giving the customers what they want, well, there's your meal ticket for life.

I just love the opportunity market. It's filled with some unique challenges, there's no question about it, and you have to get over and though them or you might just get bogged down. **There are regulatory issues, first of all, that you need to be concerned with. You have to be very careful about what you say in your advertisements, particularly when you're promising certain things.** Earning disclaimers, profit, and privacy -- it's all important for you to include it in the fine print. Or the not-so-fine print, as the case may be. There are many people out there who have gotten into serious trouble because they pushed it too far.

There's also this element out there that wants to know "The Secret" right away, when the fact is that, despite what Oprah and her favorite authors would have you believe, there is no secret. They want a miracle and they'll get mad and blame you if your product doesn't deliver it. **They want to believe that there's an instant formula to get them where they want to go, so you have to include disclaimers that tell them, very plainly, that these shortcuts won't work if they aren't willing to work hard and use them properly.** These products may help people make the largest possible amount of money in the fastest period of time in the easiest possible way, but they're only business opportunities -- not get-rich guarantees.

In this marketplace, the people who want to make the most money are the ones least likely to ever do it; that's one of the ironies of this business. God love all these people -- they keep us in business and, hopefully they get something positive by doing business with us. As I've mentioned repeatedly in this book (because it is, after all, a very important point) these people are

---

CHAPTER SEVEN

looking for miracles and they want somebody else to do everything for them. **They're not willing to do the kinds of things that I've talked about here: becoming a great marketer, working with customers, developing relationships with them, learning product development skills.** Are they more lazy than most? Are they more frustrated or do they just not understand the value of all these things? Well…a lot of them are delusional. It goes back to a story I told at the beginning of this book; I can't think of a better example.

This event occurred at the second truly expensive seminar we ever held; Russ von Hoelscher worked with us as a partner on it. We were upstairs in the hotel trying to get our game plan established when Russ said, "Look, we've been pushing this whole get-rich thing way too much. Let's really go out there to help these people -- let's just try to get them to that first $50,000 a year and show them how slowly, over a period of time, they can build that to something larger and larger until they finally they get to where they need to go." We decided that made sense, so we went downstairs and asked our attendees, "Who here wants to make $50,000 a year their very first year in business?" **Absolutely no hands went up.**

Though I accept this now as part of the reality of our business, it was like a slap in the face for me at the time. I was thinking to myself, "What's wrong with these people? Most of them have never made $50,000 a year in their whole lives -- they're like I was back in the 1980s, when I barely had a pot to piss in." But it goes back to this whole emotional thing; it's just one of the brutal realities of this business. Now, at every seminar, I ask the attendees what Russ asked them next at that seminar years ago: "Who here wants to make millions of dollars right away?" Now, as then, they all just start jumping up and down and celebrating. But they don't realize that it takes baby steps to make those millions, that there are things to learn along the way, that there's struggle and adversity to go through, that new skills have to be developed, that new knowledge has to be learned. **They're simply unwilling to go through all the things it takes to slowly get there -- or even a small fraction of those things.** Now, there are plenty of exceptions, thank God. We meet people at these seminars who are willing to work their tails off, who have realistic ideas that most of the people in the opportunity market do not.

Most people want instant cures, easy answers, quick and easy solutions. I used to think this was something limited to the opportunity market, but the truth is most markets are this way. If I had to come up with three reasons why the Dan Kennedy Platinum Group was such a wonderful life-changing experience for me, one of those three reasons would be the fact that it gave me an opportunity to meet other marketers who were selling to other markets. **It just blew me away to find out that their customers were a lot like mine, at least in this sense. Their companies were selling niche programs and books to people who weren't these delusional opportunity buyers -- and yet those people would still just put these items on the shelf and wouldn't do a damn thing with any of them.** It's as if the very act of buying something satisfies a lot of their hunger. It makes people feel like they're on the right path. They'll get into the heat of the moment and they'll go out there and spend a whole lot of money. Even if they never end up doing anything with any of the stuff they buy (which is usually the case) the very act of buying it satiates them at an emotional level.

Another challenging thing about this marketplace is the fact that it's filled with hype and BS -- there's no question about that. **But one of the reasons it's like that is because, unfortunately, that's what people respond best to.** Back in 1994 Dan Kennedy taught me that the secret is to sell people what they want and then give them what they need. That's what we strive to do. Sure, sometimes our sales material gets pretty hyped up with all sorts of

---

CHAPTER SEVEN   159

things that get our customers all excited. But for those who want to do the work, in the fulfillment products we're honest with them and straightforward about the things you have to do to make the most money. We really do try to educate people with good, solid information that will help those few who are willing to put in the time it takes to study what we offer and really put it into effect.

One thing that I've noticed recently, although I didn't before, is that a lot of people buying our products are looking to the future. When I ask customers what they've done with the stuff they've bought in the past, I often learn they're just a few years away from retirement. <u>They all honestly intend to use our materials someday</u>. These materials are sort of like an the insurance policy they mean to put effort into later, when they have the time and energy. There's no question that they're sincere.

Still, it's the programs and books that are most filled with the hype that end up selling the most and not just in the opportunity market. Lately, we've been dealing with real estate speakers quite a bit. What they sell is technically not a business opportunity -- I wouldn't look at it as such, anyhow -- but they're telling me the same thing. The things that really jazz people up the most are the hype-filled promises.

Having read through the 26 tips in the A-to-Z, Rags-to-Riches Success Formula that my wife and I used to get where we are today, I hope you'll go back and read them again, more than once. I've tried to be candid with you in every way here. I don't want to paint a false picture of our business; I'd rather be honest with you, so you can go into the whole thing with your eyes wide open and help us make this market even better than it already is.

Chapter Eight

Marketing FAQ

In the original audio program that this book was based on, this was the section where Mike Lamb asked me a rapid-fire series of questions about my business. I've included it here as a kind of FAQ, a collection of Frequently Asked Questions that we at M.O.R.E., Inc. are commonly asked. I think you'll find the answers to be instructive.

Q. **When you put out your first program, what were the feelings you got when you first started generating revenue?**

A. Power. It's just the most powerful feeling to do business nationwide, in some cases worldwide, and get all these people sending you money -- people you'll probably never meet, people who, in most cases, you'll never even talk to.

Q. **What was the biggest mistake you've ever made in marketing a product?**

A. About a year and a half ago I got myself into a terrible financial situation in which I simply over-extended myself. Most people never go far enough in pursuing their customers; well, in this case, I wanted to see how far I could go before the whole thing exploded. I was spending too much money on the front end to acquire customers -- as much as $500 to land a $50 front-end sale. It was all working for a while, but the bottom line is, I wasn't watching my numbers close enough. I do believe in going negative on the front end, given that you make all your profit on the back-end, but I should have been watching my numbers better. I exploded the whole thing and just about went into bankruptcy.

Q. **What's the best joint venture you've ever done?**

A. That would be the deal that we did with Alan R. Bechtold back in the mid-1990s when the Internet first came onto the scene. We did over $12 million in a handful of years. The timing was so perfect; the money came in faster than we knew what to do with it, so we ended up buying all kinds of goofy crap: sensory deprivation tanks, condos, and all kinds of real estate. It was an amazing time because, as far as the money went, it was just like turning on a fire hydrant. We even bought a house that we never even lived in -- we never even spent one night there. We were making so much money we just didn't know what the hell to do with it. When it's that big, it's like a drug. We were like two little kids in a candy store. I'm past all of that now; currently we're trying to do things like build our networks. But so many people I run into are doing the same thing we were -- they're just blowing it as fast as they make it because they never had any money in their whole lives and they don't know what to do with it.

Q. **So they just aren't mature financially. Let's talk about that for a second. What's the one thing you would tell anybody who's going to start coming into a lot of money?**

A. Work with a good financial advisor; pretend like you're not even making the money. Just focus on your work. Sock it away. That's my best advice. I would have millions of dollars that I don't have right now if I would have followed that advice.

Q. **I'm going to ask you two questions here; one's based on you having no money at all and the other one's based on you having $10,000. First, let's assume you lost everything that you have. You have no product library, you have no money, and you have no customers. You have 30 days, you have the phone, you have the Internet, you have a roof over your head, you have your experience. What do you do to get back on top?**

A. That's easy. I'd go immediately to all these small business people who don't know a damn thing about direct response marketing. I would put together a window envelope direct mail piece where I'd cut out the ads they're running right now, put those in the envelope, and add a little copy saying, "I can make this ad three times more profitable in the next 30 days. Open this up right now." And then I would sell them some type of consulting service doing just that. It's easy to make these ads more profitable because most of them suck. All those businesspeople are going to rip that envelope open because their ads are going to be shining up at them through the window when they're sorting their mail over the trash can. That that's the fastest way that I can think of to put tens of thousands of dollars in my pocket right away.

Q. **Okay, let's say you've got the same scenario, but you have $10,000 to start with.**

A.   I'd go to the same market I've been in since 1988 --
       the opportunity market. There are millions of people
       who are rabid for all kinds of moneymaking plans and
       programs -- and you don't even have to have anything
       put together to make money immediately. All you
       have to do is come up with an idea for a seminar or
       tele-seminar. You make them a million promises:
       you're going to get this, you're going to get that,
       you're going to get the other thing, then you go ahead
       and set the dates for the seminar. All the people start
       sending in their money like crazy so they can come to
       the event; during that time you're frantically working
       behind the scenes, so that when they do show up,
       you're able to deliver on all your promises. You can
       make a ton of money very quickly this way.

Q.   **Give me your best description of the word
       "leverage" as it applies to the business
       opportunity market.**

A.   Joint venture partners because you're able to make
       money that you never would have made had you not
       hooked up with these people.

Q.   **In your estimation, what are the criteria for
       finding good joint venture partners?**

A.   What I try to do is catch people on their way up,
       people who have lots of talent but may not be at the
       top of the game yet. Established people can be very
       difficult to get through to -- they're focused on their
       businesses and they've got all kinds of people
       protecting them from you. I love doing business
       with youngsters who have that same fire in their
       belly I had 25 years ago. I've made plenty of money

by doing business with younger people who are on the way up. I recognized that they were future superstars and then I latched on to them and I tried to do as many deals as I could with them.

Q. **What's the biggest mistake people make when working with JVs?**

A. Expecting the JV partner to do everything for you. The people who are making the most money with joint venturing do as much of the work as they can; they don't depend on their JV partners to do it all for them. When you're out there presenting to these people, wanting to do business with them, you've already got the product lined up, you've already got the sales material, you're not asking them to do very much at all. That's music to the ears of people like me. When you come along and say, "Look, I've got this sales letter that kicks ass. We're out there making money with it, the product is great, I'm willing to do all this and anything you want me to do" -- that's the best thing you can do because it gets the attention of people who are already out there doing big things.

Q. **What's your best resource?**

A. The small group of people I work with on a daily basis because they know me and I know them and we work together so well. When you work with the same talented people year in and year out, it's a shortcut to making more money. You can get so much more done in so little time, with so little effort.

Q. **How many projects have you juggled at the same time?**

A.   I usually try to have 4-5 projects going at all times, so I'm constantly juggling. Sometimes you get burned out on one, so you go to another. But I also like to have really tight , because that's the only way you end up busting your ass and getting it all done in the end. I try to set tighter deadlines, I'm constantly trying to bite off more than I can chew, I'm setting bigger goals, planning things out that we don't have any earthly idea how we're going to pull off. We plan a lot of mailings and then we set the dates with our suppliers when we're going to have the pieces ready to go, when everything is going to be ready. We set these mailing campaigns with a series of follow-up mailings and it all has to be timed right or you're going to lose money -- and then we just go to work. If it weren't for the deadlines, we wouldn't get nearly as much done.

Q.   **Do you have any public goals for the next 12 months or so that you'd like to share?**

A.   That's the thing I've struggled with on goals. I think I wrote my first goals down 25 years ago and since then I've read a lot of books about goals and, frankly, there's a lot of confusion in them. I've tried a lot of different "goal setting systems." What works best for me right now is keeping a list of the top five things I want to accomplish. Only one of them involves money; the others involve personal things that are the most important to me and I've got that list staring me in the face all the time to keep me focused.

Q.   **What do you use to put it in your face; do you just have it written down on a piece of paper?**

A.   Yup, right here where I do most of my work. It's staring at me now. It's just more of a set of guidelines than goals. One of those is financial, though: it's all about making huge sums of money and beating past performances. It's got a timeline on it. By the time I'm 50 years old, I know where I want to be financially; and I've only got four years to get there so, as they say, the window's closing in on me and I feel the pressure.

Q.   **Do you ever plan on retiring?**

A.   Oh, hell no. Never. Ever. I think retirement sucks. I hate retirement. I watch people go through it all the time, it doesn't work for them, and it won't work for me. I think being an entrepreneur is something you can't retire from because it's something that you are. It's a lifestyle more than anything and here's what I want to be able to do: the older I get, the more I want to pick and choose the opportunities I want and have the ability to say no to the others. If you want to make a lot of money, sometimes you have to be more open and receptive with these things. I want to get to a place financially where I can be more choosy. But as for retirement -- I see it as a very, very bad thing. I guess there are people that it works for, but I just don't see it as a good thing at all.

For people who retire after they've met all their goals and have plenty of financial liquidity, then sure, I think it's a great thing, but I think there are a lot of people who are too driven to retire and I think you and I are in that category. Entrepreneurs love to play the game and all this is about more than just work. It's about challenging yourself; it's about doing things that you're passionate about, that interest you greatly. Like Dan Kennedy said, the only way to successfully retire is to have something to retire to, not from. I see so many people who hate their jobs, who hate what they're doing for a living, and dream of retirement. I have a good friend who had a high-level position with the government, who traveled all over the world and managed hundreds of people -- and he hated his job. Every single day was filled with dread and he counted down the days until he could retire.

When he finally did retire, at the tender age of 53 (because he was making big bucks), he decided he was going to play golf the rest of his life. Well, after 6 or 8 months, he was 40 pounds overweight and his skin had turned this awful color. Now he's back to working again, he's lost all of that weight, and he's looking trim and slim. He's 62 years old, but he's the model of health and he's happier than he's ever been in his life. I think that so many people who hate their jobs should quit them right now. They should find things they can do that they have a passion for. Life is too short to go to a job that you hate.

Q.   What are your favorite sayings?

A.   I have this quote Dan Kennedy gave me called "Little hinges swing big doors," and I love that visual analogy. I think life does boil down to little things that can make a big difference. Another of my favorite quotes is, "It's better to have it and not need it than to need it and not have it." That 'it' could be anything: money, time, or other resources. One more quote I really like is "The same problems that cause some people to break down cause other people to break records." You see so many people who are like, "Oh my God, I'm so stressed out! I can't handle it!" but that same amount of stress just bores the crap out of other people. It's not so much what happens or what your life is filled with; it's all about your ability to handle it.

Jim Rohn says, "Don't wish that your life is easier; wish that you were better." That's another great philosophy I've adopted because 15 years ago I was in a situation that almost gave me a heart attack. There I was, in my early 30s, and I was actually having chest pains because I was so angry at certain things happening in the business. Those same things can happen to me these days and I don't even get fazed by them. The same thing that used to tick me off for a whole day now ticks me off for ten minutes.

Q.   What's your favorite quote about focus?

A.   Again, the quote from Dan Kennedy that was once hanging in my office; now it's hanging in a building here on the property. It says "Distractions abound; we must fight for focus." The best thing I ever did was to get a manager for the company after Eileen stepped down from the company as President and CEO. I went over there and tried to run it for a couple of years, but it was a disaster -- I was unhappy and me being in charge wasn't good for the company. For all those years she ran the company, all I did was focus on the marketing: product development, promotional stuff, and the like. Now

---

I've got a good, strong, solid general manager in there running the company, and I'm back to working at home again, doing the things I love, focusing on the things that bring in the money. I see too many businesspeople trying to wear all the hats in their businesses. They're working so hard, but they're not getting a thing done when it comes to revenue building or profit generating. Too little of their time is spent on the things that could be bringing their company so much more money.

Q. **What's a secret about you and about your business that we won't hear anywhere else?**

A.   I'm obsessive, compulsive, I'm a total workaholic, and I work 14 hours a day most of the time. I don't know if it's something to be proud of, but it is what it is. I'm very driven and I'm very ambitious and that can be a good thing -- but it can also be a major burden.

Q. **What do you like to do when you're not working?**

A.   I don't ever not work. I have different kinds of work for the different periods of the day. At nighttime I've got a laptop computer and I'm sitting next to my wife and half-watching some stupid TV program and enjoying some quality time with her, but I'm also reading my email or working on re-writing certain projects; things that are relaxing and creative. At other times of the day, when I have a lot of energy, I'm writing sales copy and things that require a certain mode of thinking or certain state of mind. If you want to crank out sales copy that'll get people jazzed up and excited, you have to be excited, too. Then at nighttime, when you're more relaxed or in the afternoon when you're having a low period, you can go back, think about what you wrote, and carefully re-write it.

So I'm always working. To me, the work is a good thing. I envy people who are more balanced; I really wish I could be like them sometimes. Then again, I don't think that I'd be writing this book if I were a more balanced person. I don't think I would have ever achieved anything of any significance.

Q.   Are you involved in any hobbies?

A.   The work is my hobby -- therefore, is it really work? You know, for years the people who love me have been trying to get me to work fewer hours. They keep saying, "Come on, T.J., relax, smell the roses." What they don't get is that, for the most part, I love what I'm doing. Now, it's not all fun and games. When you're challenging yourself the way I do, you'll have days when you say, "Oh my God, what am I doing here?" But the truth is, it's rarely that bad. You hear stories about how artists, musicians, and actors are dedicated to their craft and the ungodly amount of time they spend at it and the price they pay for their art...and people respect that.

But when they find out some entrepreneurs do the same with their businesses, oh man, that's a terrible thing! We're workaholics -- people feel sorry for us, but they don't feel sorry for the people in other professions who give it everything they've got. I'm really sensitive about that. For years I tried to fight my "workaholistic" nature. I was convinced that it was a bad thing. Now what I try to do is channel it into work that's truly fulfilling. It's my sincerest wish that people are going to get some good, life-changing value out of the things I'm trying to share here.

Q.   What do you do to relax?

A.   I have work I do in the evenings that I find very relaxing. I think, for me, the hard work is entertaining family members that I have nothing in common with, except that we all came from the same family line. They have no clue what I do or, at least, they don't understand it. And, frankly, I have no clue what they do, either. To me their lives look boring -- and to them my life looks like too much work.

Q.   What's the favorite part of your job?

A.   Product development gives me the most satisfaction. I love to develop product. I love to come up with ideas and turn those ideas into informational products. I enjoy all those things you have to do to create the product -- not just the actual work of writing sales copy, but also coming up with the hooks and the angles, the themes and the concepts. When it all comes together and you make a ton of money, there's no better feeling in the world. I think product development is a very therapeutic thing and I try to spend a significant portion of every single day doing it.

Q.   What's your least favorite part about the business?

A.   Working with the accountants. No offense to my

accountants, but I hate looking at the numbers because of what they represent. If I sit there and focus on it I can get in tune with the numbers, but to me it's almost like a foreign language; my brain doesn't work that way. To me it's a necessary evil; you do it because you have to do it. But I've got myself surrounded with people that I trust and respect. I tend to just look at the bottom lines and, as long as the bottom lines are healthy, then I just keep charging forward.

Q. Who is the person who has most influenced your business life?

A. My wife. She's the one who turned it around for me. She came along and encouraged me, in the beginning especially. Her managing skills bolstered the business for all those years when she ran the company and let me develop my marketing skills and abilities. I will always be indebted to her for that.

Besides her, it's Russ Von Hoelscher. He was the one who opened the door for us. He's more than a joint venture partner -- he's somebody I care deeply about. If it weren't for him, none of this would have happened the way it did happen. When we met him, he had over 20 years of experience; he saw something in us and I'm trying to do the same thing now with the people I meet in these seminars and other events, the folks who are just like I was 20 or 25 years ago. I'm trying to do for them what Russ did for us: he gave us a leg up.

In the process he helped himself too, of course, but that's the way business is supposed to work. I like it that way. I like the whole win/win nature of it. Other than Russ and Eileen, Dan Kennedy would be the person who has meant the most in terms of helping us make more money. Dan's a marketing genius and we were so fortunate to be part of his Platinum Group.

Q. **If you had a marketing secret you could put into a time capsule for people 50 or 100 years from now, what would it be?**

A.   That's easy: two-step marketing. The real secret here is to do things to separate the smaller group from the larger group, so you can then spend more money on that smaller group of more qualified prospects. The goal is to make an initial sale to them that will lead to a series of lifetime sales. This method is old as the hills -- everyone's been exposed to it. The best examples are companies that tell you to call this toll free number or go to this website to receive some kind of a free item. It lets people come to you; then you offer them some type of an initial report. DVD, CD-ROM, audio CD, print, it could be anything -- some information package they pre-qualify themselves for by requesting it. Even more important than that, now they feel that they're the ones that came to you, not vice-versa. They forget, of course, that you're the one who had the ad to begin with.

You see, people don't like to be sold things; they don't like to be high-pressured. What they do like, though, is to buy things. It makes them feel good, especially if they have a hunger for what it is you sell. That's the way all these business opportunities are. People love to look for things that are new, things that are interesting, things that are hot. They want to get involved in something at the right time. If you offer them a free CD or report showing them the greatest newest discovery, they'll come to you. That's the best way you can build a list of customers who buy from you initially and then continue to buy from you for many years.

Q. In what ways do you feel that you're making a difference in people's lives?

A. That's a tough one. Sometimes I'm not sure I am. I know I'm helping the people I work the closest with, since they adopt a lot of the ideas I teach them. Some of our customers can be real fickle; one minute they love you, the next minute they hate you. John Lennon was killed by a man who was a fan of his. Customers can be that way, too. They can be fans one minute and the next minute they'll hate you. The people I know I've made a real impact on are my former customers who are now my joint venture partners, who continue to work with me on a regular basis.

Q. Let's say I'm a customer who likes what you're doing for them. I'd like to take that next step and want to be a joint venture partner. What do I do?

A. I've got customers who just keep showing up at my seminars and, whenever one of my partners like Russ Von Hoelscher has a seminar, they go to those events too, so I just keep running into them everywhere. Pretty soon we exchange email addresses, so we're emailing back and forth and they know I want to help them above and beyond all of

---

the different programs we sell to them. So I'm looking out for them and trying to continue to find ways I can do more for them so they can do more for us and we can work together. Jeff Gardner is my best example of that. Usually, the only customers you hear from are the ones who are complaining. The rest of them are out there doing things with what you're selling, so for the most part they're too busy to sit there and write you letters saying, "God, I love you guys! I love what you're doing!"

And yet Jeff Gardner was that type of person; he was writing us letters telling us how he loved our programs and how much money he was making. This was a pleasant change from the complainers, so one day I decided to give him a call and I learned he only lived a couple of hours from us. At the time, he was going to school at Kansas State University, so I invited him over for a seminar. We got to know each other over a period of time and got to working together and liking each other. Hey, that's all a joint venture is! It's just two people who like each other enough to start doing business together. They have mutual interests, they're both passionate for their businesses, and they're both serving the same markets -- so, naturally, they want to do more business with each other.

You know, the money is great. But what's really great is having the money and also doing business with people you really enjoy, people who have the same interests and are moving in the same direction you are. They understand you in ways other people don't -- to them you're just a weird duck. The entrepreneurs I know are dancing to the beat of a different drummer. Their lives are about a whole lot more than just grabbing a paycheck and job security. I've got enough family members who have the employee mentality, and I'm around enough other people in my own company who have the same mentality, so I know there's a distinct difference between them and us. Their wants and needs are very different.

Now, obviously, if you're going to run a company, you need people like that. Those people are the salt of the earth. When I go through periods when I'm totally burned out, when I've pushed it too far, I envy the hell out of these people. I wish I could shut it off and get away from it all sometimes -- but I can't, really. I can't be them and they can't be me. When I first became self-employed, back in 1985, I used to think that everybody should be self-employed; I was like one of those born-again Christians who want to save everybody's souls. Now I know better. I see a lot of people who are self-employed that probably shouldn't be. I also think there are people who are destined to be self-employed and to be entrepreneurs -- but at whatever moment in time they're in right now, it may not be right for them. They still have a little way to go on that employee mentality journey. They're too security-minded; they're so used to all the years of conditioning that this whole idea of working for things that interest you and getting involved in projects that excite you doesn't make sense. Those things are foreign to them.

Q. **Looking back over your business career, what's happened to you that has taught you the most or**

that has had the greatest effect on your business?

A.   There's this conversation I had with Russ von Hoelscher a few years into the business that keeps coming back to me. I was going through some tough times; this was in 1993, when our initial promotion quit working for us. It had been bringing us millions of dollars and everything was great -- and then bam, it stopped working. They don't last. That's the heart-breaking thing; you can go from having a hot promotion to wishing you had a hot promotion all in a matter of months. I was depressed, wondering how we were going to get out from under those problems, and Russ told me, "T.J., just remember that the real business isn't over there at 305 East Main in Goessel, Kansas. The real business is you and your ability to understand the marketplace and to be able to craft products and services that are right for that marketplace."

I was so worried about all the things that had to do with the physical part of our business and Russ helped me realize that that's not really the business. The real business is in our knowledge of the marketplace, our ability to continue to give that marketplace products and services that it values. That was a major lesson for me. Every time I'm going through tough times -- like the time twenty-two months ago, when I almost went bankrupt -- that phone call keeps coming back to me. That was the best advice anybody could ever have given me.

A friend of mine who's an Episcopalian priest tells me that you should have an attitude of gratitude at all times. So, a few months ago, I took that to heart and sat down and wrote down all my personal assets, starting with my own creativity and imagination. It was a very cathartic exercise; I literally wrote down everything that I have possession-wise and intellectual-wise and everything meaningful in my life that I can call a personal asset. It was truly amazing. I included people that I do business with; I included friendships. Now, whenever I start to get depressed or it looks like things aren't going right, I go back to that list and look it over and, sometimes, add to it. By now it's a pretty large list; it includes some goals and other ideas, but for the most part it's everything I have, everything I am. It's amazing to see how much I've amassed. I think if you performed this exercise, it would really give you a different perspective on who you are, what you have going for you, and what you can use to propel yourself into another stage of your life. I think it's meaningful because you look at your own list and think, "I forgot I knew how to do that," or "I forgot I had that."

One of my quotes here says when you count all your assets, you always show a profit; people tend to forget that when they get down. One of the things Dan Kennedy taught me was this: "You have to work on yourself every bit as hard as you work on your business." You have to sit down sometimes, do your self-work, count all your assets, look at the big picture. You need to remind yourself of all these things and keep your attitude as positive as you can, talking to yourself in the most positive ways. One of my favorite quotes (which I forgot to mention before) is, "What you say to yourself about yourself is the single greatest thing."

Epilogue

Everyone reading this book has his or her unique story. You have your own distinctive set of talents and abilities and you have your own list of assets to make. You've got a chance to dive right into this wonderful market where millions of people are searching for opportunity. Those people aren't just searching for money; that's not really what they want. **What they really want are all the things they think that money will buy. It's not so much a desire for money, but to have all the great things in life.** These people share an outrageous hunger and it's your role to fill it. This isn't meant cynically. To do well, you really have to understand these people and be willing to try to help them. They're going to spend that money no matter what; so they may as well spend it with you than with some fly-by-night promoter who's going to hurt them in the end.

I encourage you to go back and read through this book, repeatedly, because what I've tried to do is just remove all of the filters, to be real with you about what it takes to make huge sums of money and enjoy a lifestyle that most people will never experience. **The closest they'll ever come are with those hobbies that thoroughly engross them, where they'll spend hour after hour on something that they really passionately love to do.** That's about as close as it gets to some of the things I've been talking about in this book.

I know that so many people out there are so close to hitting it, so close to achieving their dreams, but they walk away before that happens -- and they don't even realize it. The people who keep getting up every time they get knocked down are the ones who succeed. When you talk to super-successful entrepreneurs and you get them to tell you about their pasts, you'll find that they went

---

EPILOGUE

through an enormous amount of adversity. **I once read a quote that the average entrepreneur experiences 4.5 business failures before they finally make it.** I don't know if that statistic's accurate or not, but I'll bet there's some real truth in it.

I was watching a television show recently called "Mind your Own Business" in which they were interviewing a restaurateur who has four different restaurant chains. He said that at one time or another, he'd had 24-27 different businesses -- and all but those four had gone into the drink. Well, that's not unusual. Dan Kennedy once told me about a very successful client of his who made millions and finally retired the way he wanted to. When Dan first met him, he went into the guy's office and saw, behind the guy's desk, this huge bulletin board covered with business cards. Dan said, "Oh, I see you collect business cards," and the guy said, "No, those are all from my businesses at one time or another." The guy had been involved in so many different things over the years, achieving various levels of success. Finally, with the help of Dan Kennedy, he ended up making tens of millions of dollars within just a few years -- and that's the way a lot of entrepreneurs are.

Sometimes people think they're failing, but they're really not. What they're really doing is acquiring experience; it just feels like failure because things don't work out the way you want them to. **The only real failure is when you finally get kicked down and you refuse to get back up again.** When you finally give up on your dreams and say, "I'm never going to try that again," that's when you're a failure.

So often, what's most painful is also what instructs us the most in life. We learn from a lot of the adversities and challenges that we face and live through. That's how we become stronger, more capable, and more competent than we already are. They say that success occurs when preparation meets opportunity. Well, sometimes the only way to get really prepared for the big things, the things that can make you tens of millions of dollars within a short period of time, is to go through as many different things as you can. **Some make you money, some don't, and some kick your ass. You achieve some victories along the way, but then, finally, all the elements fall into the right place at the right time and, just like that client of Dan Kennedy's, you're able to get involved in one big deal that's life-changing.** You're able to use all the experience you gained over the years to trigger that big payday, when millions of dollars just come raining in on you.

So don't give up on your dreams. Keep going forth, keep moving forward. If you'll do that, ultimately the question is not will you get rich but when will you get rich and how rich will you get? Because it's going to come.

There's no entrepreneurial superhero out there. Entrepreneurs are just people who kept trying. Like everything else, it was often three steps forward and two steps back for them along the way. Whatever real confidence and skills they have, whatever true abilities they have, were all developed because they kept moving forward, continuing to do things like setting higher goals, always trying to do more in less time, trying to challenge themselves, trying to take on more projects than they could comfortably handle, trying to continue to work harder and smarter and set bigger goals and constantly bite off more than they could chew. **It's through all those pressures that our greatest skills are formed. Sometimes that development doesn't feel very good, but it is good because it toughens you up**. It's like going to the gym every day for an hour or so. After a while you'll develop those buns of steel, those six-pack abs. In business, when we go to the "gym" every day, when we accept bigger challenges, when we continue to push forward, when we set higher goals and continue to be willing to do what everyone else is unwilling to do -- it transforms us.

EPILOGUE

It's amazing to me when I see somebody out there who announces that they've generated $2,000,000 in revenue from a business and all these other people gravitate to that person, as though they're the next big expert, the next big guru, the next big thing. **All they really did was add a little more consistency, a little more action, a little more thought and intelligence to their business, and that's what made the success happen.**

The nice thing is, the further you go and the more successful people you meet, the more you realize that there's nothing special about them. They're just people who had a dream and enough courage to move forward. One of my favorite quotes is this: "A big shot is just a little shot that just kept right on shooting." That's the way it is with all of the super-successful entrepreneurs, from Bill Gates on down. **You find out that they're people who continue to move forward in spite of the obstacles; they set bigger goals and challenges and they refuse to quit.** Along the way, they developed the skills, the knowledge, the experience, and the resources they needed to succeed. But they did it slowly, over a period of time, by continuing to move forward and refusing to give up.

You have to keep going: you can't look back, except to reminisce and see what you've done wrong and learn from it. Otherwise, there's no reason to look back. The bottom line is this: all the money is great, but you'd give it up in a heartbeat if you had a sweet little grandchild that you loved more than life itself and somebody had a gun to their head demanding your money. You wouldn't have to think twice. All the money in the world doesn't mean a thing when it comes to something like that. **It's the other things in life that are the important.** It's surrounding yourself with people that you really like and respect, people you enjoy working with. It's the challenge of setting these goals and seeing how far you're capable of going and falling in love with marketing and all the things I've talked about in this book. **Those wonderful things really do give you a deep sense of satisfaction. The** money is the icing on the cake, a by-product of all of that, a way of keeping score.

I got a video not too long ago from a friend of mine who said "Hey! I just wanted to let you know that my program's working and I did over a million dollars in revenue last year." He did it by selling information products through Click Bank. I looked at that video and thought, "He's doing all the things I'm doing. He's focused on them, he's doing them en masse and he's doing them consistently. He's not letting anything get in the way of generating revenue for his little niche products online and last year he did a million dollars in revenue."

Now, let's go back to that quote Dan Kennedy gave us at one of our meetings. I put it in a nice picture frame and hung it up on my wall, and I've mentioned it several times here already. It just says: "Distractions abound; we must fight for focus." **There are only so many hours in a day, even for people who have a lot of energy. The older you get, the less of that you have and the faster time moves; so focus is very, very important.** Putting the maximum amount of your time and effort into those few things that will bring you the most amount of money is what will make you rich.

The guy I was just talking about a few paragraphs back is a normal, everyday guy. Everyone is, when you get down to it -- even Bill Gates or the President of the United States. **They're all people who continue to move forward in spite of all the obstacles and they develop certain skills that help them along.** Admittedly, the skills they've developed are exceptional. That's the whole thing: they're not necessarily special, but the skills, the knowledge, the experience, and the talent they've developed most certainly are. All these are within your reach if you're willing to just go out there and work hard and get them.

I hope that if you've invested in this book you'll be willing to read it more than once, and will think very carefully about all the ideas I've tried so hard to express to you here. Our marketplace is extremely lucrative. **Use the ideas I've shared with you to gain a real familiarity, an intimate knowledge, with this market and get started today.** I hope to meet you in person someday and discuss your success. I love meeting someone who tells me that something we sold to them really did make a difference in their life. It's a lot more about you than it is about us, after all -- that's one of our success secrets.

Find the companies in this marketplace that are doing the best, the ones that are making the largest amounts of money. Look for handful you like the most and become a good customer of theirs. **Get on their mailing lists and start receiving everything they offer because that's the only way you're going to really get on the other side of the cash register and understand how this business works.** When you look at it from a business point of view more than as a consumer, you'll realize that there are common denominators here -- that all the companies in the opportunity market serve the same basic type of customer and they're all looking for the same basic types of benefits and advantages. The amount of creativity here is vast and it all serves the same type of person, so get familiar with the market by becoming a good customer. **If you're already a customer of the opportunity market, you already have a lot more familiarity with this market than you realize -- and that's another secret of our success.**

There's plenty of room in the opportunity marketplace for anybody who wants to practice the methods that I've shared in this book and, in so doing, to make millions and millions of dollars along the way.

I would encourage you to get involved in this market -- so that I can meet you, get to know you as a friend, and do business with you in the future.

CPSIA information can be obtained at www.ICGtesting.com
Printed in the USA
LVOW061820030413

327457LV00001B/183/P

9 781933 356051